New Economy Emotion

The New Economy Excellence Series

New Economy Emotion:
Engaging Customer Passion
with E-CRM

Alfredo Zingale
and
Matthias Arndt

JOHN WILEY & SONS, LTD
Chichester • New York • Weinheim • Brisbane • Singapore • Toronto

Other Wiley Editorial Offices

John Wiley & Sons, Inc., 605 Third Avenue,
New York, NY 10158-0012, USA

WILEY-VCH Verlag GmbH, Pappelallee 3,
D-69469 Weinheim, Germany

John Wiley & Sons, Australia Ltd, 33 Park Road, Milton,
Queensland 4064, Australia

John Wiley & Sons (Asia) Pte Ltd, 2 Clementi Loop #02-01,
Jin Xing Distripark, Singapore 129809

John Wiley & Sons (Canada) Ltd, 22 Worcester Road,
Rexdale, Ontario M9W 1L1, Canada

British Library Cataloguing in Publication Data

A catalogue record for this book is available from the British Library

ISBN 0-470-84135-4

Typeset in 11/14pt Garamond by Mayhew Typesetting, Rhayader, Powys
Printed and bound in Great Britain by Antony Rowe Ltd, Chippenham, Wiltshire
This book is printed on acid-free paper responsibly manufactured from sustainable forestry, in which at least two trees are planted for each one used for paper production.

This book is dedicated, with love,

to Annette, my better half, who contributed steadfast
encouragement and time I would have otherwise spent with her,
and also to Laura, cheerful friend, who instigated the idea of the
book in the first place
Alfredo Zingale

to Bernhard, unquestionably the best grand-father in the world
Matthias Arndt

'In the morning sow thy seed, and in the evening withhold
not thine hand: for thou knowest not whether shall prosper,
either this or that, or whether they both shall be alike good.'
Holy Bible, King James Version, Ecc. 11:6

CONTENTS

Any book written about the Internet, particularly about marketing on the Internet, risks being out of date the moment it's published. Web-based technologies and e-marketing techniques are continuously evolving. There seems to be an ever-growing number of Internet companies that introduce new technologies for speed, bandwidth and security, new performance software and new Internet services – all of which are aimed at sustaining the extraordinary growth of e-business around the world. This growth also spurred a debate on the 'new economy' versus the 'old economy', where most of the attention was focused on the flamboyant 'pure Internet plays', on the dazzling dot-coms' IPOs, on the 'clicks versus bricks' start-ups. The hype was that the future was to be found only in the new economy, typified by extraordinarily young and dynamic entrepreneurs who, unencumbered by old-economy baggage, could raise venture capital, 'flip' their dot-coms and make unbelievable fortunes. The meltdown of the Nasdaq at the end of 2000 signaled that the hype had fizzled out, leaving many people to wonder what had happened to the 'new economy'. What happened is that some old-economy reality had finally caught up with the new economy. As stock valuations have come down drastically throughout the technology sector, the expectation is that only those Internet companies with a real portfolio of intellectual property, real profits and real customer relationships are likely to survive and thrive. Those with merely a business model are likely to run out of cash.

Old-economy reality also applies to marketing on the Internet. Those companies that are market focused, have a competitive value proposition and continuously strive to improve their customer relationships are more likely to leverage their presence on the Web to their advantage and achieve leadership positions. Those that remain product focused, don't make the effort to know their customers and don't invest in customer relationships are less likely to reap the benefits of the Web – they are more likely to be relegated to the ranks of the 'also ran'.

Even though the hype has fizzled out, the Internet-based new economy has generated new business paradigms that have changed the competitive landscape for many old-economy companies, sometimes without their realising it. What is the role of marketing in the midst of this change? Indeed, does it have a role? How is marketing being affected by all of this?

We think that marketing has a major role to play at this time of change. We hope to bring some insights by recognising some visible trends and patterns in the use of the Internet that affect the marketplace and the business models of many industries. We also hope to help readers turn marketing into a more competitive and value-creating activity for their enterprises by applying Web-based technologies to age-old marketing challenges: establishing a dynamic presence in the market, engaging prospects and customers in relevant communications and building lasting and profitable relationships with customers.

This is not about taking a narrow, incremental view of marketing, nor about down-playing or limiting the potential offered by the new technologies. We simply believe that customer focus is central to any enterprise that wants to acquire and keep a leadership position and that the Web offers a unique capability for achieving and maintaining such customer focus.

Marketing professionals, none the less, have the responsibility to demonstrate to their management that they know how to deploy the latest technology profitably in their own environment, in areas where the potential benefits are highest and where they can gain a visible advantage for the company. This is what we hope to show our readers, for example, when we work through the scenarios of personalized web sites and e-mail marketing campaigns.

We intend to address those managers and entrepreneurs who have boards of directors, who are asked for profits and growth every year if not every quarter, who have some old-economy baggage to carry (distribution networks, inventories, legacy systems, bricks-and-mortar infrastructures) and who value on-going relationships with their customers as a key component of their business success. Their challenge is to make the transition from the 'old' to the 'new' economy, from traditional marketing to Web-intensive marketing, without losing sight of their customers and without losing focus on their business performance. We hope that they will find this book relevant.

Marketing and the Internet

CHAPTER 1

Overview

In this chapter we present:

- Trends and developments that are having an impact on marketing strategies and on the way companies think about the big picture.
- The challenges, both old and new, faced by e-marketing.
- The total customer experience as a model by which to understand and build long-lasting customer relationships.

The Internet: a unique phenomenon

Three aspects of the Internet make it a unique phenomenon, whether we look at it as a media, a technology or a utility:

- The speed by which it is adopted by consumers and businesses on a global scale.
- Its ubiquity, that is, the fact that it can be accessed just about anywhere at any time.
- The access to practically unlimited content that is mostly free.

At present the existing, growing and developing technology infrastructure, wired and wireless, is providing almost unlimited access – the Internet is always on. In the future the expected exponential growth in computing power and network bandwidth will encourage the development of rich content and interactive user interfaces well beyond those experienced so far, making the Internet the preferred medium for transacting information.

The Internet reaches people at work, in the home, at educational institutions, at cybercafés. And through WAP (Wireless Application Protocol) and future G3 telephone technology, the Internet will reach people anywhere they happen to be. According to the Internet Industry Almanac report of 25 October 2000, the number of worldwide Internet users at the end of 1999 was estimated at 280m, 40 per cent of whom were in the United States. Internet users are defined as any persons over 16 years of age who uses the Internet at least once a month. The US, however, ranks only fourth in terms of penetration, or number of Internet users as a percentage of the population. Canada, Sweden, Finland, the US and Iceland, in that order, were the countries with the highest Internet penetration (over 40 per cent) at the end of 1999. They were followed by Denmark, Norway, Australia and Singapore in the 30–40 per cent range and by New Zealand, the Netherlands, Switzerland, the UK, Taiwan and Hong Kong in the 20–30 per cent range. While by the end of 1999 there were nine countries with over 30 per cent Internet penetration, by the end of 2002 there would be eight more countries joining those ranks: Austria, Belgium, Germany, Ireland, Israel, Italy, Japan and South Korea. At that time the US is expected to have close to 60 per cent penetration, or 165m Internet users, but it will account for only 27 per cent of the total 601m Internet users forecasted worldwide. Internet growth is going to remain robust for several years according to these projections, as penetration rates continue to increase in countries around the world.

Today consumers are buying PCs primarily to access the Internet. Hence, the growth of Internet usage is largely a function of the penetration of PCs in the economy and of the deployment of the telecommunications infrastructure. The potential for Internet usage growth is very high in the largest European economies and is more likely to be realized in the short-term as the EU, national governments, telecom operators, ISPs (Internet service providers) and content aggregators address the main issues affecting Internet growth in Europe.

According to a Forrester Research report, the following issues needed to be addressed in 1998 in order of priority: telecom deregulation, attitudes to technology, infrastructure, multilingual/multicultural demands, access cost, EU regulatory environment, national regulatory environment and PC penetration. In 2001 the top three were forecast by the same report to be multilingual/multicultural demands, attitudes to technology and infrastructure.

In Europe the main issue affecting Internet usage growth is therefore going to be the availability of content that can satisfy the needs of a diverse, multilingual, multicultural environment. A number of European Internet start-ups, including Europe Online, AllEurope and Scandinavia Online, have begun to address these needs on a pan-European or regional basis in cooperation with local search and directory services and content providers.

Whichever way you look at the Internet, as a technology, a medium or a utility, content is and will remain the main factor affecting Internet usage.

An enabling and disruptive technology

While there are many ways to look at the Internet, we view it primarily as an enabling technology with the potential to create new paradigms for businesses.

The growth of the Internet, as we saw from the statistics and projections above, is nothing short of phenomenal. A United Nations *Human Development Report* looked at the number of years it took a major new technology to reach 50 million users, generally regarded as the widespread acceptance threshold. It found that the radio took 38 years, the personal computer took 16 years and the World Wide Web took just 4 years.

This sort of growth is causing several changes to traditional business models, whether business-to-consumer or business-to-business. It alters the economics of business and it creates new opportunities and threats. It brings prices down and it creates demand for a higher level of customer service. It lowers barriers to entry for new market participants and it raises barriers to existing ones. It causes disintermediation (the removal of intermediaries from the value chain) and it creates new intermediaries. It facilitates the quick build-up of preference for new brands and it exposes the weaknesses of existing brands, as consumers can more easily and quickly make comparisons in terms of service, choice and value experiences.

All of this suggests that enterprises should not view the Internet as merely a new medium or a new channel (although both of these could be starting points for internal discussions), but more as a disruptive technology that demands a strategic response. In other words, enterprises should formulate an Internet strategy for all aspects of their business: marketing, distribution, inventory management, procurement. The place to start with is marketing, because customers are the driving force behind the growth of the Internet.

The Internet and business success: what has changed

In the early 1990s, Michael Treacy and Frederick D. Wiersema (1997) identified three strategies or 'value disciplines' of business success:

- Product/service leadership – product/service performance or uniqueness.
- Operational excellence – no-hassle, speedy service, low cost.
- Customer intimacy – personalised service, commitment to total solution.

There was a time when excelling in one of these value disciplines was sufficient for a business to gain a leading market position and maintain competitive advantage. But now, as competition is being sharpened by communication and information technology, businesses are required to excel in all three disciplines to become and remain leaders in their field.

Most companies understand the need for innovative products in order to succeed. Some also understand that they need to increase Internet investment in their customer-facing activities in order to achieve higher degrees of customer intimacy. Few, however, realise that by doing so they also increase the demands and pressure on their back-office functions and systems to perform according to the expectations of customers, who are now better informed and more exacting than ever before. Customers in the new economy expect choice, quality and Internet speed. Therefore, companies in the new economy need also to excel and compete in operational and process capabilities, which may require additional investments in back-office processes and infrastructure, whether owned or shared through strategic partnerships.

The Web: a dreamed-of marketing tool

In this book we will use the term e-marketing, rather than Web marketing or Internet marketing, to describe marketing activities that are enabled by the Internet and other Web-based and electronic technologies.

For most marketers, the Web is a dreamed-of marketing tool. A company can advertise its brand and products or services, inform customers and prospects of new products and other new developments, offer promotions and discounts, enable the ordering of products and services and settle trans-actions – all through the Web. The Web is also the tool that has made it possible to implement economically and efficiently two of the more significant marketing ideas of the last decade, namely relationship marketing and one-to-one marketing.

Regis McKenna's *Relationship Marketing* (1991), Don Peppers and Martha Rogers' *The One to One Future* (1993) and *Enterprise One to One* (1997), together with Frederick Reichheld's *The Loyalty Effect* (1996), contributed to a greater understanding of what it takes to move from mass marketing to customer-centered marketing and how to acquire and retain profitable customers.

While the concepts behind relationship marketing, one-to-one marketing and customer loyalty are not new in an absolute sense (they have been practised by inspired business people on a small scale probably throughout history), it took process thinking and information and communication technologies (ICT) for them to become applicable in the context of larger enterprises. This is analogous to the process thinking and ICT deployment that has allowed production and back-office processes to move, for example, from build-to-stock to build-to-order environments.

E-marketing: where is it coming from, where is it going?

So, where is marketing headed? What are the challenges and opportunities of moving to e-marketing? What is changing, what is different, what is remaining the same? A brief look at what happened to marketing in the past may help us infer some directions with regard to the future.

Mass marketing

Mass marketing was the earliest form of marketing in the industrialised world. It was driven by the economics of mass production, where goods and services were produced and distributed in large quantities to the market with no choice, or limited choice, for the consumer with regard to looks and features. This 'one size fits all' mindset was also applied to media communications that were broadcasting unidirectional messages to the consumers.

Segment marketing

Segment marketing or target marketing developed in the 1970s and early 1980s with the arrival of the minicomputer followed by the personal computer. These two developments propagated the use of IT throughout the enterprise by moving it out of the glass-enclosed, mainframe computer room into the hands of business professionals. Customer knowledge began to be integrated into the design of products and services to fit the needs of specific customer segments. Marketing communications followed, with more specialised messages and media addressing these customer segments.

Database marketing

Closed-loop database marketing grew from the application of accessible database technology to direct-response marketing in the 1980s and early 1990s. Customer information databases held not only demographic information, but also buying patterns, transaction information, product usage and other data. Updating and maintaining customer information became key to the accurate delivery of segment-sensitive and time-sensitive communications to the customer base, closing the loop with every customer interaction. Technology enabled the beginning of a dialogue between suppliers and customers.

One-to-one marketing

One-to-one marketing was born in the 1990s and is, in the ultimate sense, marketing to segments of one, although in practice it addresses segments of a few with very similar characteristics. One-to-one marketing carries segmentation, interaction and customisation to a finer degree of resolution by establishing a continuous dialogue with customers. The concept was very appealing, but it couldn't be implemented by enterprises in a practical and consistent manner until Web technologies came into play. Now, some of the features offered by the Web such as interactivity, tracking, personalisation, customisation and e-mail, coupled to customer information, make it possible to establish an on-going dialogue and even a learning relationship with large numbers of customer segments or even individual customers.

The Web offers a technology platform unequalled so far in terms of pervasiveness and flexibility, which can be used to build trusting relationships between customers and suppliers. That in turn should translate into additional and more profitable sales for suppliers and into more rewarding experiences for customers. The challenge for e-marketing is to turn this potential into reality.

The challenges for e-marketing

According to Philip Kotler, Distinguished Professor of International Marketing at Kellog Graduate School of Management, the mission of marketing has been and still is to acquire, keep and grow customers, where by 'grow' he means increasing over time the amount of business gained from each customer. This mission is clearly aligned with the more general objectives of growth and profit of any enterprise. To fulfil the mission in the context of the new economy, the e-marketer may need additional skills related to the new electronic media. However, even the most skilled e-marketer will not be able to fulfil this mission entirely unless the whole enterprise is market focused, not only the marketing department.

Market focus and value propositions

Being market focused is *not* selling the catalogue or whatever is coming off the production line, is not asking customers what they want and blindly doing whatever they ask, is not emulating competitors or even leap-frogging them with a better product.

A successful market-focused enterprise does three things particularly well:

- Develops an imaginative understanding of customer needs for each market segment it serves.
- Formulates a superior and profitable value proposition for each market or customer segment.
- Organises itself into one or more value delivery systems that impeccably fulfil and communicate the propositions to the customers.

In other words, the value proposition drives every function and activity of the enterprise, not just marketing or sales. Does this sound too idealistic or unreal? Dr Lynn Phillips, founder of BMFO LLC, Building Market-Focused Organizations (www.bmfo.com), argues that among all the alternatives available to deliver value, the market-focused perspective is the most realistic way to make money.

A value proposition is basically a promise to a customer or set of customers of specific value experiences in return for buying into a relationship with the supplier. In a business-to-business context, for example, this requires suppliers to have a detailed understanding of how customers do whatever they do in order to offer the products and services that help customers achieve quantifiable gains in output and quality. This in turn leads to greater revenues and profits for customers and repeat sales for the supplier.

The challenge for an enterprise is to offer superior value propositions in each of its businesses or brands. To achieve that, a company needs to formulate the desired experiences and their value to customers in comparison with competing alternatives.

Businesses that have adopted a market-focused perspective and formulated a value proposition have usually concentrated their attention on the delivery of value experiences through their products or services – an experience delivered against a price charged – but often stop there. The product or service is the vehicle for that experience. However, businesses deliver value experiences to their customers and prospects well beyond their products and services, through the multiplicity of contacts that customers and prospects have with different customer-facing activities or with partners of the business (sales, marketing, support, distributors, customer service etc.). Each of these experiences, with different points of contact, including the Web, may positively or negatively affect the customer's net impression of the business. As the value delivery concept is extended from fulfilment of product and services to the entire set of contact points with customers, businesses have begun to place a growing emphasis on understanding and managing the 'total customer experience'.

Understanding and managing the total customer experience

The total customer experience is the effect on the customer's judgement of all the impressions received while interacting

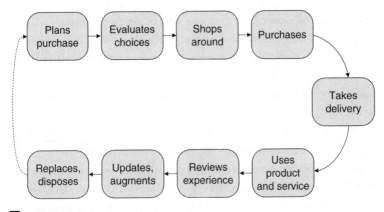

Figure 1.1: The customer buying process

with the vendor during the buying process. The customer's buying process is the series of events that they go through from the time a purchase is planned to the time the purchased product or service is disposed of or terminated.

One of the more useful ways to understand the total customer experience is to map the customer's buying process for the particular product or service (see Figure 1.1). Typically, customers go through the following events in the buying process:

- Plan a purchase.
- Evaluate alternative choices of brands, products or suppliers.
- 'Shop around' for the best deal.
- Decide to purchase.
- Take delivery.
- Use the product or service.
- Review their experience.
- Update or augment.
- Replace or dispose of the product or service.

The supplier's process is also described against the customer's buying process: for each of the events, the desired customer experience is described and the entity or department responsible for delivering the experience is identified (see Figure 1.2). Articulating such experiences in a plan is the first step for clearly defining roles and responsibilities and for assigning tasks to the different customer-facing entities involved.

The next step, often a challenge for the business, is to obtain internal agreement on the ownership and the performance measures associated with each value experience. After that come execution and monitoring of results. That is in essence the process of understanding and then managing the total customer experience.

In the context of a large business where there are several intermediaries between the customers and the business or where contact points are spread among several departments or entities, it is clearly not easy to execute such a plan faultlessly. It takes motivation and commitment on the part of the people involved, beyond the aspects of process design, content design and information technology, to ensure that the promise of value is consistently kept across organisational boundaries.

Managing the total customer experience remained an almost unattainable goal for most companies until the arrival of the Web and its related software technologies. The architecture of a web site and its related databases can be designed to provide a communication platform for all of the company's customer-facing activities. Dynamic custom-isation, an appropriate multimedia environment and mean-ingful content can be applied to deliver desired experiences to customers whether they are gathering information towards a new purchase, searching for opinions and references from a community of users, trying to place an order or planning a replacement. And what do customers expect? To begin with, they expect choice, quality and speed.

If it is information they are looking for in your site (researching topics/issues is the largest Internet usage

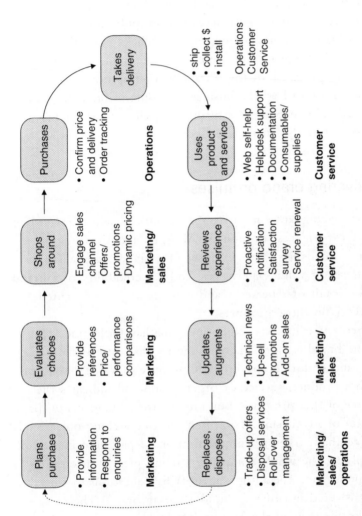

Figure 1.2: Supplier's process vs customer buying process

category), they want it on media that are appropriate to their environment (often a bandwidth issue), they want content that is relevant to them and up to date (this is the single most important value to deliver and a profiling issue), they want information that is easily accessible in 'pull mode' (straightforward navigation and few 'clicks') and that is reasonably frequently delivered in 'push mode' (e-mail typically). Because of the Web, e-marketing now has the opportunity to lead the business not only in the definition of desired value experiences throughout customers' buying process, but also in their delivery.

Delivering brand promises

As more companies improve their ability to deliver rewarding value experiences through the Web, competition among brands intensifies. The promises of a brand are essentially promises of value experiences, and the credibility of a brand is the result of repeatedly and consistently well-executed delivery on those promises.

Scott Ward, Larry Light and Jonathan Goldstine (1999) define brand as 'a distinctive identity that differentiates a relevant, enduring and credible promise of value associated with a product, service or organization and indicates the source of that promise'. Building a strong brand is not just a matter of advertising. Too often this overarching objective is left to the marketing communications department instead of involving the whole company; a brand plan is, after all, a business plan. The authors identify five questions that need to be answered in order to build a strong brand. These are applicable beyond the high-tech world.

The first three questions have to do with value delivered by the product or service itself:

- What are the features and measurable characteristics of the product or service carrying the brand name?
- What are the benefits to the customer resulting from those features?
- What are the psychological rewards or emotional benefits received by using the brand's product or services?

The last two address the key values and attributes impersonated by the brand that differentiate it from other brands and that attract and retain customers:

- What are the deeper values reflected by the brand to the targeted customers (achievement, family, personal freedom, community etc.)?
- What is the personality exhibited by the brand (friendly, caring, contemporary, conservative, aggressive, trustworthy etc.)?

Answering these questions can be a revealing exercise for an enterprise whose brand or brands have evolved without a deliberate effort on the part of the company and without a top management commitment to deliver the promises of the brand through the entire customer experience.

Performance shortfalls in the area of customer satisfaction and, eventually, in financial performance can be related to gaps in the understanding of the total customer experience and to the attitude and behaviour of the people in the organisation towards the customer.

From an e-marketing point of view, it is important that both the presentation style and the content of the web site reflect to the target customers the personality and the values of the brand, but it is equally important that the web site be designed to provide access with the right functionality to all the customer contact points, to reinforce the benefits expected from the branded products and services. Hence, it is important to integrate the Web not only in the communication plan of the company, but also in its operational plan.

Building lasting customer relationships

The interactivity offered by the Web and the dialogue that can occur there between customers and suppliers make it the ideal medium to build relationships and increase customer satisfaction and loyalty. At least, this is what we are led to believe by those e-marketers that pronounce relationships, satisfaction and loyalty in a single breath.

It is true that e-marketing is primarily about relationship marketing, a topic we will cover later in more depth, but it is also true that customer satisfaction and customer loyalty are two different things and not always related to one another. Plenty has been said and written about customer satisfaction and there is hardly a company today that is not measuring customer satisfaction in some form or other. There is also abundant literature describing the benefits associated with customer loyalty, at least from the perspective of the supplier. Loyal customers are more likely to repurchase and more likely to recommend the brand. They are less price sensitive; they do less 'shopping around'. They require less service, generate higher profit and in general are a lot easier to work with. But how do you know that? How do you measure it?

Too often, loyalty is only thought of as an attitude and is measured as such: 'propensity to buy' and 'propensity to recommend' are two typical indicators of customer loyalty in many surveys. This would place loyalty at the same level as satisfaction, which *is* an attitude. Measuring satisfaction, for example, doesn't say anything about how your customers perceive your value compared to your competitors'. However, customer loyalty is more than an attitude, it is a *behaviour*, and the best way to measure it is to relate it to repeat purchase behaviour.

This is, of course, more difficult to do than running attitude surveys, because it requires gathering and analysing purchase history data and, whenever possible, profitability by customer. This probably explains why fewer companies measure loyalty than measure satisfaction.

The paradox in the satisfaction/loyalty equation, however, is that high customer satisfaction does not necessarily translate into repeat purchases. A dissatisfied customer can remain loyal because of a *de facto* monopoly situation, inertia or lack of information when facing apparently undifferentiated offers. On the other hand, a satisfied customer can display disloyal or defector behaviour because of the abundant availability of choice, plentiful information, self-confidence in the decision-making process and general scepticism about brand promises. In other words, satisfaction is a necessary but not sufficient condition for loyalty.

Similarly, customer satisfaction is not a sufficient condition for customer profitability. Frederick Reichheld (1996a) said that 'what matters is not how you keep your customers but how many satisfied *and* profitable customers you keep'. If the customers you want to keep are the profitable ones, then you should have some measure of profitability by which you can segment your customer base and identify the profitable ones.

The next question is how you keep them. The answer is by making sure that they continuously receive value from the relationship with your company – value that is commensurate with their standing in your segmentation scheme and with their expectations.

Most companies have some sort of segmentation scheme by which they rank the relative 'importance' of their customers. However, few companies knowingly allocate their marketing resources among their customers according to their relative ranking. The result is that all customers receive more or less the same value, whether that is information resources, special offers, customer services etc. Consequently, the higher-ranked customers (their most valuable customers) are under-served compared to the lower-ranked ones, thus raising the risk that they may ultimately defect to the competition.

From the supplier's viewpoint, customer loyalty is not just a warm and fuzzy idea, it is a matter of economics: it has been said that acquiring a new customer is at least five times more expensive than getting business from an existing one. Another fact is that marketing resources are limited and need to be allocated where they obtain maximum return, typically among the bigger and more profitable customers. This makes sense. But there is a flip-side to this argument. For customers, loyalty is a two-way street – they are loyal to you if you are loyal to them. All customers, whether big or small, profitable or unprofitable, think that their purchase is important and expect to receive value superior to what is offered by the competitive environment. Providing superior value is, after all, the goal of all companies aiming at market leadership positions. Companies therefore have a complex balancing act to perform between fulfilling the promises of their brand for the market at large and keeping their most profitable customers. Fortunately, this is an area where e-marketing can make a significant contribution.

As the Web becomes the main marketing infrastructure, several technologies of increasing sophistication (from database driven, to intelligent agents, to collaborative filtering, to rule based) are available to deliver high levels of personalisation and customisation to satisfy the needs of different customer segments and individual customers. Later we will see that, even without making use of sophisticated technology, it is possible to conduct effective relationship marketing on the Web as an important step in a customer loyalty or retention strategy.

Establishing a dynamic presence in the market

On the Web, establishing a dynamic presence in the market means promoting your web site by linking it to other web sites that are visited by your target market. You can register your site in the appropriate categories of directories and search engines. The best known are all US Web properties: Yahoo!, Lycos, Infoseek, AltaVista etc. They are all global in reach and some have editions in other geographic locations.

There is plenty of literature on how to ensure that suspects and prospects can more easily find you when using search engines. You can add meta tags in your site that include attention-getting keywords, descriptions and titles that are used by search engines to index your site. You can also separately register each product or service that has its own page on your site. These and other tactics are discussed, for instance, in *Dan Janal's Guide to Marketing on the Internet*.

An emerging approach for gaining new business is to establish collaborative marketing agreements with other web sites that offer complementary products and services, whereby the partnering sites refer to each other URLs and share revenue for referred business. In business-to-consumer markets this approach is also called affiliate marketing and works like this: when a visitor clicks through from an affiliate web site to the destination web site and buys something, the affiliate site is granted a commission. In the e-tail business, affiliate marketing programs have been applied by companies such as Amazon, CDnow and Dell and are growing in size and sophistication.

Measuring results

Measurement and analysis of web site traffic is the first step towards measuring response and estimating the ROI (return on investments) of your web site. A great deal of traffic data is collected by web server software in log files that can be analysed through available web analysis tools and techniques. 'Access log files' collect the IP addresses (identifiers) of computers that come to your site with file names, date and time. 'Referrer log files' collect the URLs (addresses) of other sites that link to your site. So it is possible, with some degree of approximation, to answer questions such as:

- How many visitors came to my web site?
- What content or pages have they seen and in which order?
- How much time did they spend?
- Where did they come from?

'Visitors' are not real people because web logs don't track people but rather computer Internet addresses. A visitor is a unique or de-duplicated session that a visiting computer has had on your site: the number of visitors is obtained by counting the number of different IP addresses in the log file. Inaccuracies are introduced, for example, when several people use the same PC or when subscribers of online services access the Net through the same gateway computer. But, however imperfect, the analysis of log file data is essential to test web pages, to measure response to promotions, to understand or discover visitors' interest in certain topics versus others or to assess the effectiveness of links to other sites. All this is information that can be used to continuously improve the performance of your web site and the return on your investment. Since web traffic measurement is a rather technical and rapidly evolving subject, it is best to call on a web professional to select the right measurement tools and services.

Relationship marketing on the Web

CHAPTER 2

Overview

In this chapter we discuss how and why:

- Content has become a key value to be delivered by e-marketing.
- Companies find ways to improve their business results with the help of the Web.
- Customer focus and Web-enabled customer relationships are key to e-CRM.

We previously said that the mission of marketing is to acquire, keep and grow customers. We also said that the purpose of a market-focused business is to deliver customer value experiences that fulfil the chosen value proposition. These values experiences encompass not only those delivered by the product or service supplied by the business, but also those delivered by the different points of contact with the customer in the supplier's organisation and in the business partners' organisations. What additional value should marketing contribute as organisations move to relationship marketing on the Web?

The additional value delivered by marketing

From a strategic point of view we could, therefore, say that marketing should:

■ provide the architecture of the total customer experience, i.e. the map and definitions of the customer value experiences across all customer contact points;
■ act as the catalyst, with top management back-up, to achieve agreement across organisational boundaries for the delivery of those value experiences.

This is quite a tall order for marketing, but within reach as the Web becomes the marketing infrastructure for the business. Marketing must also deliver its own value in order to acquire and retain the loyal and profitable customers demanded by its mission. That value is both the dialogue *and* the content. Together, they constitute the base of a fruitful relationship with target customers.

According to an Internet Track survey of European usage of the Internet, 86 per cent of respondents use it to research topics and issues, 77 per cent to obtain information about products and services, 62 per cent download software, 50 per cent receive news and updates and only 25 per cent access the Web to purchase products or services online or offline through traditional channels. Clearly, having rich, relevant, up-to-date content on their web sites is a must for e-marketers. E-marketing is relationship marketing and content is king.

Content is king

Content, however, has not been a major preoccupation for marketers in the past, other than for market research. Marketers have typically been measured on the delivery of events (campaigns, trade shows, customer events, press events etc.) and on outcomes (brand awareness and preference, incremental revenue growth, business leads, event attendance rates and so on). When it comes to creating marketing messages for those events, it is often the task of PR or advertising agencies to extract content, sometimes painfully, from their marketing clients. But now the creation and delivery of content have become a must for e-marketing.

Many competing web sites are available to your customers and the time they can spend browsing is limited. If you want your customers to keep coming back to your site and become regular patrons, you must provide personalised content that makes your site a preferred resource. What kind of content? To start with, there should be content that fulfils the needs of the customer throughout the buying cycle. Put yourself in the customer's shoes or, better, put your hand on your customer's mouse and try to answer the following questions:

- Can customers find information and structure that make it easy for them to understand and choose your products and services?
- Can they find the closest distributors, store locations or available inventory?
- Can they find special offers that are suited to their environment?
- Can they easily place orders online or offline?
- Can they find tips or application stories to extend the use of your products and services and thus increase their satisfaction?
- Can they find after-sale support information, frequently asked questions, updates?

These questions relate to just some examples of the more general, public domain information for which customers look. However, even in the case of public domain information, not all customers are equal nor should they be treated equally – you have the opportunity to provide some level of personalisation. Suppose you are going through a product roll-over, introducing a 'hot', new product to replace another one that you want to make obsolete. You prepare an announcement that emphasises the new product's 'cool' features and technical capabilities and you make it available on your web site to all customers who purchased the previous product. Will all these customers react enthusiastically? Some will and some won't.

The 'early adopters' among them, those who want to own the latest cool stuff, will be eager to read the announcement and ready to buy. But the 'followers', those who only buy stuff that has been proven in the market, may have a different reaction and ask themselves questions like: My current product is doing just fine, why is it being obsoleted? What will happen if I don't buy the new one? Will I still get support and under what terms? These customers need reassurance. So if you know your customers' attitude to technology, you can craft different messages with regard to the same product introduction event. And your web site can deliver the right messages to the right audience by using customer profile information, personalisation options and flexible content management features.

Content integration and aggregation

In addition to the public domain content generated by the front-end or customer-facing departments, valuable content is generated by the back-end systems in the enterprise. This is information that is unique to a customer and is generated after a purchase: order status, receivables, applicable discounts etc. Because it is administrative in nature, marketers tend to disregard its value and don't think about making it available in a personalised web site, but it can make a significant difference.

Customers can immediately get non-assisted web help on topics and information that are important in their day-to-day work; they don't need to go through sales reps or customer service agents who may not have direct access to the back-end systems. Even if they do, a personalised web site that can deliver this type of information to your customers will free up the time of your reps and agents for more productive tasks. However, the integration of front-end and back-end content for individual customers requires integration between the web site and the back-end systems. Later on, we will discuss how personalised web sites and e-mail marketing processes can be integrated with back-end systems and processes to deliver even greater value to the customers.

There are other content services that you can aggregate to your site to enrich your customers' experience. For example, you can host on your web site a community of users of your products and services who exchange experiences and, therefore, benefit from their combined, accumulated knowledge. You will benefit too, as online communities are a major source of low-cost market research information.

You can provide access to information about complementary products and services offered by your business partners. This offers the opportunity to extend your market reach and to develop revenue-sharing marketing arrangements as business partners link each other's web sites and refer to each other's products and services.

You could also provide access through your web site to a rich array of other information to match your customers' preferences and lifestyles: travel, culture, sports, financial news. This is not far fetched because you do not have to build this content on your own. You can buy syndicated information from many outside providers and package it in a way that distinguishes you from your competitors.

If your customers can find content in your site that is not matched by your competitors and is unique, because it is generated by your back-end systems, then the competition is further than 'a click away'.

The pivotal role of content management

What is emerging from the above is the need to think of content as a central part of the value provided by e-marketing and, by extension, we need to think possibly of a 'new' e-marketing role: online content management. This goes beyond the role of the webmaster who technically administers the web server and other system components. This role is about creating and aggregating content, which is relevant and valuable to target customers, and about keeping it fresh. It requires the insight of a journalist, the business discipline of an editor and a great deal of enthusiasm and dedication, particularly when it comes to extracting information fit for publishing from internal company sources.

The decision about what content to offer from your web site should be tested against your value proposition. It should consider the size of your market (how many of your customers use the Web), your customers' expectations about the value to be received from your web site and the level of personalisation to be offered to your most valuable customers.

Global, local or both?

To say that the World Wide Web is a global medium should be a redundant statement. Potentially anyone anywhere, any customer or prospect with an interest in the products or services of your company, should be able to find you and establish a dialogue with you through the Web. They will, of course, also find your competitors and they will draw their own comparisons.

One thing they will notice is whether you are global or not in your approach. Perhaps the scope of your business is not exactly global in the sense that it addresses the whole world, maybe you address only a specific number of countries. None the less, once you are on the Web you should be able to project your company image, convey relevant information and establish dialogue with customers and prospects in any one of the countries you address in their language, not just in the language of the company management.

English (in some form or other) is, of course, the main language on the Web and likely to remain so. Countries with high English fluency have required less content-localisation cost so far and have been the initial target of the large US web properties (Yahoo!, Lycos, Infoseek etc.). But, in the global economy, countries with low English fluency represent an equally significant and growing market opportunity. The trend in the large portals has therefore been to provide local-language editions to satisfy the demand for local content.

Globalisation, however, goes beyond the issue of translation and localisation of content in different languages. Being global, from a brand and relationship marketing perspective, means that:

- you take ownership and responsibility for the relationship (content and dialogue) with your customers anywhere in the world;
- you have a strategy that includes and involves your local sales channels in managing the relationship, rather than delegating it to them by default.

This is not a new problem and it often caused friction with sales channels around the question of 'who owns the customer?'. No one does, of course. Customers, if they are not deprived of choices, choose to do business where they receive most value. None the less, the debate remained because the issue was control, not relationships. However, with the arrival of the Web, more power with regard to the relationship has been shifted to customers and controls have been 'disintermediated'. Now you can develop content once, manage it from one place anywhere in the world, establish a dialogue with your customers in any way they choose and facilitate customers' relationships with the local sales channels. The new economy, more than the old, demands that marketing think global and act local.

What's your reason for being on the Net?

Patricia Seybold, noted e-business consultant, described the evolution of e-business in five stages:

- Providing company and product information.
- Enabling customer support.
- Supporting electronic commerce.
- Personalising interaction.
- Fostering community.

This scheme also helps understand why companies want to be on the Net: the first three stages have to do with improving the performance of the company, the last two with improving customer relationships.

Many companies go on the Web initially with the idea to save costs in marketing and sales and to gain incremental business, in other words to improve their own performance. Improving customer relationships, retention and loyalty may be a distant objective at this stage. That is fine. Your presence on the Web and the value you want to deliver to your customers and prospects should be built gradually, one step at a time, starting from the first goal of providing company and product information. However, in doing so you should not lose sight of the ultimate goal for being on the Web, which is to build long-lasting customer relationships.

Convey information about company, products and distribution

Let's start with the first step: provide company and product information. This is not merely a matter of displaying brochures on your site. Experience with traditional print brochures shows that most tend to convey a sales pitch in some form or other and few answer the customer's questions. Translating your brochures into html, the language of web sites, is not a successful e-marketing practice.

Prospects and customers want to find out who you are, what you do, how they can benefit from your offer, where they can find more information, how they can buy etc. To be a successful marketing tool, your web site should be organised to answer those questions in a way that is aligned with the sequence typically followed by the prospect or customer. It is the latter who is in control, who initiates the action and who expects to find answers by interacting with your web site. Here we need to go back to what we said earlier about the total customer experience.

In this step the objective is to deliver the desired customer experience at the beginning of the customer's buying cycle. To achieve that, the best way is to ask several of your customers what they want to find in your site and how. The collected information will help generate the site map and the functional specifications for designing your web site. Then it's a matter of building it, populating it with the requested information and letting customers test and critique it.

By focusing on useful information and incorporating customer inputs in your design, you are more likely to have, in the end, a web site that delivers the desired customer experience. The visual aspects of the site (layout, logo, fonts, colour schemes etc.) are also important and should reflect your brand identity, values and personality. However, all aspects of graphic design should be balanced against the site functional specifications, such as loading speed, ease of navigation and readability by most browsers. Complex graphics, photos and animation may look great, but they take an awfully long time to load and may end up frustrating the visitor. Reputedly, most people won't wait more than 15 seconds before switching to another site. Hence, the trend is away from busy layouts and complex images towards simpler layouts with relatively few, colourful blocks or headlines linked to other pages.

Reduce cost of selling

Providing useful, easily accessible information about company, product and services on your web site is a way of saving money in marketing and sales during the pre-sales part of the buying cycle, particularly business to business. It helps reduce the number of mail shots involved in direct marketing campaigns and it can also reduce the number of queries that customer sales and service reps would normally field. Nevertheless, this is not automatic. Customers need to be educated to go to your URL (your web site address) and 'pull' the information they need rather than depending on direct mail or on customer calls by phone or travelling reps. This can be done by prominently displaying your URL on all print communications and then gradually reducing content to headlines and summaries, inviting customers to go to your site for more information. Next, customers can be invited to opt for e-mail rather than print, thus reducing the need for direct mail to a few, specific marketing events. Later we will cover the entire e-mail marketing process and see the possibilities it offers.

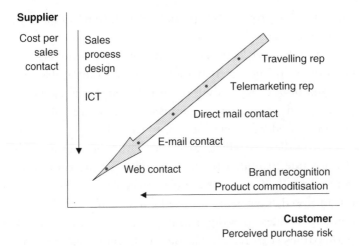

Figure 2.1: Selling cost vs purchase risk

More generally, however, the opportunity of reducing the selling cost of any one product or service is a function of lowering the risk perceived by the customer in making the purchase decision. Periodically buying the same high-value item from a known brand is a low-risk decision compared to choosing a low-cost but critical OEM (original equipment manufacturer) component for a product under development. But more often the risk is correlated to the price and complexity of the product or service, which is illustrated in Figure 2.1.

A high-risk purchase decision may require one or more customer visits by a sales rep. A low-risk decision may only require confirming the price by e-mail. The cost per sales contact comes down each time by almost an order of magnitude as we move from a traveling rep visit to a telemarketing rep call, to a direct mail contact, to e-mail. What brings down the purchase risk perceived by the consumer are primarily product commoditisation and brand recognition. What drives down the cost per sales contact are primarily sales process design and information/communications technology.

The purchase risk of certain categories of products has come down far enough that they are now commonly purchased online. According to an Internet Track survey, the top five product categories purchased online are software, PCs and related products, books, music CDs and games. Clearly, for these product categories both the purchase risk and the value provided to the consumer by the traditional retail and resale channels have diminished to the point where the traditional intermediaries are being 'disintermediated' by the new e-business paradigm in large segments of the market.

Companies such Dell, Amazon and CDnow became market leaders and established strong brands in a short period because they focused on customer intimacy – they applied web technologies and customer information management to achieve undisputed leadership in that dimension in addition to achieving operational excellence. Their advantage was that they didn't have to integrate e-business into an existing business model, they started with it.

If your company is not in one of these product categories, you still have the opportunity to reduce the cost of selling. By using the principle illustrated above, you can match the appropriate type of sales contact to each of the product or services in your offer according to the purchase risk perceived by your customers. This requires you to know how customers perceive the risk. You may think, particularly if you are in business to business, that customers will always ask for a sales rep, the most expensive form of sales contact, no matter what they buy. In fact, most customers want to save time for themselves. Sales calls are time consuming and, for low-risk decisions, they would be perfectly happy to gather information from your site and interact via e-mail.

In the case of large accounts, where you may have repeat orders under the same purchase agreement, a personalised e-commerce solution may be preferable from the customer's viewpoint to having to deal with a sales rep. On-going sales support and occasional customer enquiries could be handled by an inside sales rep. The account sales manager you would have hired for such an important customer could then provide real value by managing high-level, face-to-face customer relationships and by developing new business in the account.

To sell or not to sell online

If you already have a channel structure, the decision to establish a new online sales channel is a strategic choice of the first order; it is not a tactical decision about cost or incremental business. It affects your company's existing channels and distribution strategy and you should be carefully considering the pros and cons. You should ask questions such as:

◆ What market space does the online channel address?
◆ What products and services will it deliver?
◆ Does it compete with existing channels and where?
◆ What additional value does it bring to the customer that the current channels don't provide?
◆ What additional customer service, customer information management and logistics infrastructure will it require to be competitive?
◆ What level of marketing investment will be needed to establish its brand identity and the necessary brand awareness?
◆ What incremental business and/or savings will it generate and when?
◆ Do we have the skills to build it and manage it?

Ranjay Gulati and Jason Garino (2000) examine the question of whether to integrate Internet business with traditional business or keep it separate. Their finding is that the key to success is *how* you carry the integration. The benefits of integration come from the leveraging of shared resources such as customer information, purchasing and logistics and from operating under the house brand. So, if you have decided to build an online channel and consider you should keep it totally separate, you should think again, the authors say.

Increase the productivity of your sales channels

If building a new online channel is not your immediate goal, another alternative could be to increase the productivity of your traditional sales channels by leveraging the one-to-one marketing possibilities offered by the Web together with customer information.

As we said before, customer information is essential for establishing dialogue with your customer base, and selling to the existing customer base is much more productive than selling to new customers. For example, by knowing who your customers are, what they have purchased and when, it is possible to recommend specific and conveniently priced trade-up offers and complementary products and services that are more likely to be bought. This is not new, it is basic database marketing applied to up-selling and cross-selling. But, when executed through the Web, it allows a much higher degree of personalisation and interaction at purchase time, which leads to better results.

This one-to-one dialogue does not have to disrupt the relationship that customers have with the existing sales channel, it can co-exist with it. Reseller locator software on your site can help customers find the closest outlet for the special offer they found on their personalised pages or received by e-mail.

Synchronising marketing campaigns with the reseller channel is of course a must, so that they have the inventory on hand for the products offered, or have quick access to it. But the main challenge is to obtain the cooperation of reseller channel partners for sharing their customer information with you. Not all of them will do this for fear of losing control over 'their' customers, even though the benefits of cooperation, in terms of incentives and additional business leads, are made clear. Start with those who want to cooperate, prove that it is a win—win situation, promote the results and others will join in.

Attract new business

What about attracting and generating new business through your web site? Isn't this a valid objective? One way to try to answer the question is to draw an analogy with a trade show. There are some similarities between being present with a booth at a trade show and being present with a web site on the Net. At least, there are similarities among the questions you may ask. How much walk-through traffic stops at your booth to see what you've got on display? What do they show interest in? How many see your ads announcing your presence at the show? How many are referred to you by your marketing partners at the show? How many individuals fill in a registration card? How many of those 'suspects' become prospects and, eventually, customers? And so on.

Your trade show people will tend to have optimistic answers to those questions before you make the decision to spend the money to go, and so will your web marketers. But the clinching argument usually is that all your competitors will be at the show and you simply cannot afford not to be there. It is the same for having a strong presence on the Web.

Here is where the analogy ends, because the virtual world of the Web has some clear advantages over the physical world of any trade show. It is not limited by time and space, so your web site is (or at least should be) on 24 hours a day, 7 days a week, and the content it can display can be virtually unlimited. It can be designed and promoted to generate and increase traffic from the desired target markets anywhere in the world, and it can be continuously improved through the growing number of tools and services available to measure and analyse web site performance.

Close new business with direct response

To attract new business, your web site should be thought of and designed as a direct response device rather than as a glossy magazine, primarily for three reasons: the Web, with its text-based interaction and hyperlinks, is particularly well suited to direct response; bandwidth is still a relatively scarce commodity for most users; and direct response is the most efficient method for structuring interaction so that it leads to the desired conclusion: the order transaction.

Web site design should be concerned more with the architecture of the information and how users process text on the page than impressing visitors with large photos, fancy graphics or animation, all of which gobble bandwidth and slow down response. The organisation of information should be as flat as possible, with most of the choices available on the home page to minimise the number of clicks. Every page should be clearly identifiable as part of your site and should be tested to see if it supports the direct response intent of the design.

 IMPLEMENTATION CHECKLIST: direct response marketing

Direct response marketing has been around for some time and its process steps are well known:

- Segment the market and select the target market segment.
- Create and promote an offer that compels the target market to respond.
- Measure, measure and measure response.
- Qualify, qualify and qualify new business leads.
- Deliver qualified business leads to the sales channel.

One general condition that applies to direct response marketing is that all direct response designs should be tested before going into production. This is particularly simple for Web-based direct response. Separate URLs can be set up for different offers and the response rates in number of hits can be measured for each URL to determine the most successful offer. The closer an offer is targeted to a customer segment and the more appealing it is, the higher will be the response rate.

Having defined the best offer, the next step is to design the interaction with the web site: visitors are asked to take a series of actions that qualify their interest, move them from suspect to prospect status and lead them to a close. Examples of actions are: find more about the product or service, download a demo, specify intended use, add to shopping basket, have a sales rep call, buy the product or service.

All offers or promotions have a limited lifetime. The frequency with which new offers are introduced and promoted is a function of the target market and of the level of activity on the web site. In consumer markets they may change daily, in business to business it may be monthly. What is important is to continue to test not only the offers for direct response effectiveness, but also the different sections of the web site that invite interaction and dialogue with visitors so that the entire site works well as a direct response device.

A direct response web site must support dialogue with real people not just with 'visitors', that is Internet addresses in server log files. The web site therefore needs data about real people. In its simplest form, for example for low-risk purchases through an online sales channel, real customer data is collected through order forms. For more complex purchases, prospect data is collected through registration forms in order to support the dialogue that will convert the enquiry into a purchase. Depending on the value of the products or services involved, the enquiry qualification process can be carried out by telemarketing staff before forwarding the now qualified leads to sales. Whether the leads generated from the web site are fed directly to a sales automation system used by the sales reps or simply e-mailed, what is important is that they first be qualified with a procedure agreed with the sales organisation. A quick turnaround time is important – 'cold' leads are dead leads, but consistent lead qualification is even more important for the credibility of the marketing department.

Expand your ability to serve customers

The Web together with other electronic media can help you enhance and extend your customer service, sales and communication capabilities in a multiplicity of ways. Here are some of the possibilities.

Customer service agents in call centres can use the Web to answer customer enquiries and refer customers to appropriate product information on the enterprise's web site. Interactive voice response units could announce the appropriate URL for the information corresponding to the customer's selection. The online shopping section of the web site could offer a 'call-me-now' button, so that a customer can have a sales rep call back at the time the customer is ready to make a purchase and only needs a little clarification. Product demonstrations or training sessions can be held for your most valuable customers by combining phone conferencing with the Web: customers dial a phone conference number, listen to an audio presentation synchronised with visual aids or demonstrations presented on the Web. Simple product presentations or demonstrations can be designed to be self-running on the web site and activated by visitors. Conversely, for more complex products, outbound telesales reps can call business prospects for an online demonstration and a question and answer session.

In the communication area, traditional print ads, press releases, brochures and other presentation materials should point to specific web addresses for further information. Clear and easy-to-remember listed links help readers navigate directly to the suggested web page and find the additional information. Conference papers and other printed documents for distribution should display the URL where the electronic versions of the documents are available for distribution, downloading and local printing. Similarly, all commercial web sites could offer visitors the possibility of downloading electronic brochures or receiving text-only versions by e-mail.

What we see is complementarity between the Web and other media or communication channels, not substitution. As the radio did not replace newsprint and television did not replace the radio, so the Web will not replace other marketing media. What is changing fast, nevertheless, is the role of the different media relative to one another, and their respective budgets as the Web takes more space and as more of the business world goes online. So, take a strategic approach to your customer communications – integrate the Web into your communication mix with the objective of serving your targeted customers better while keeping communication expenses within your planned cost envelope.

Shorter time-to-customer

Time-to-customer, a dimension often associated with the logistics of a business, is also very important in the communications area. How long does it take to deliver your marketing messages to your prospects and customers using traditional media? Excluding the time to write copy, lead times for traditional media are several days if not weeks. Electronic media offer the possibility of reducing this time to hours. In addition, they offer the possibility of defining with much higher precision what content should reach which target group.

In theory, you could use any medium to address small groups of individuals, or even specific individuals if you knew enough about them. In theory, you could write copy and place an advertisement in the right publication at the right frequency to reach just one specific individual. In practice nobody does this, because the cost per contact would exceed any acceptable level and make it impossible to justify from an ROI viewpoint. Traditional media are best used when addressing target groups or market segments made of large numbers of individuals. The Web offers the opportunity to target small numbers of people or even individuals through personalisation features not available in traditional media. This is why we prefer to say 'time-to-customer' rather than 'time-to-market'. Short time-to-customers is particularly important to ramp up sales and achieve targeted profitability on a new product, e.g. let your customer know about your new product before the competition announce theirs. It also helps your customers receive important information on time so that they can do their job better or improve their quality of life.

Later in the book we shall see how the Web and e-mail marketing can help you bring down your time to customers and address selected individuals.

Relationship marketing is customer centric

Today customers have more choices and businesses have more competition than ever. Building valuable, long-lasting customer relationships is even more critical to the success of the enterprise and has given rise to extraordinary interest and new developments in CRM, or customer relationship management.

Under the impetus of software developers and consultants, CRM has become a practice that provides tools and business processes to coordinate the multiple points of contact between the firm and the customer. CRM is a practice that should help manage the total customer experience we described before.

Web-based tools and processes are the most effective for CRM and have retained most of the attention of e-marketers, but the Web is only one of the media that customers can use to contact a company, even though it is fast becoming the most popular. There is the phone, fax, e-mail and regular mail and there are sales people who can leverage face-to-face contact to build personal relationships.

Software vendors offer a wide range of applications to support an enterprise CRM environment. Most of the applications fall in the categories of sales automation, marketing automation and service automation and offer technology to implement call centres, personalised web sites, e-mail marketing, campaign management, multiple channel integration or e-mail response management. In addition, they support the activities of sales reps, telesales reps and service engineers as well as sales, marketing and service management. Few software vendors offer the full range of solutions; many companies specialise in focus areas. Annuncio, Broadbase, BroadVision, Brightware, Chordiant, Cisco, E.piphany, MessageMedia, Net Perceptions, Nortel, Oracle, PeopleSoft, RadicalMail, TIBCO, SAP and Siebel are just a few of a large number of software vendors.

The multiplicity of customer contact points adds the challenge of retrieving information about customer experiences across organisational boundaries in the enterprise. Yet it is precisely customer information that marketing professionals need to improve the total customer experience and build lasting customer relationships. The tough question to answer in relationship marketing, therefore, is: what do you know about your customers? What knowledge does your company have about its customers that can be shared across all customer contact points to improve the total customer experience? How do you capture it, how do you analyse it, how do you act on it, how do you keep it current?

Customer information management

The questions above are related to a different practice to CRM, CIM or customer information management. Customer information management is not about information technology, it is a content management practice that deals with one of the most important assets of a company – customer information, whose purpose is to maintain and improve customer relationships and generate new business.

In the 'new economy', intellectual property and customer relationships are the two most important assets of the enterprise. In 'old-economy' thinking, no matter how well an enterprise is equipped with modern technology, customer information is delegated by default to the IT department and customer relationships are what sales people are supposed to maintain. The consequence is that customer data is gathered only to support internal administrative processes such as order processing, billing and shipping and is collected in different information silos defined by business processes.

Such data is typically inadequate to support relationship marketing and cannot be easily accessed. Worse, there are probably coding inconsistencies and duplications that make it very difficult to aggregate data for single customers. This is not the fault of IT, whose mission *is not* to manage content or to improve customer relations. Its job is to deliver and ensure the operability of systems that support the vital business processes of the enterprise. Rather, it is the responsibility of marketing to define the customer information needs for customer relationship management, independently of where the data is collected.

One major requirement in customer relationship management is that, once registered, the customer should be consistently recognised at any contact point in the enterprise. This requires stringent customer ID standards to be enforced on all applications that capture customer information. Few things are more irritating for a customer than having to enter the same registration data every time they enter a new application.

Depending on the size and history of the enterprise, customer information can be stored in a single database or spread across a number of legacy databases. However, once linked through a unique customer ID, customer information can be analysed through a variety of measurement and analysis tools to support business decisions.

What customer data should be kept in CIM databases? The answer is the minimum required to do the task. Customer data is a perishable commodity, it must be regularly maintained and updated and that costs money. Companies disappear through mergers and acquisitions, people change jobs and move. Also, the rate of information decay varies with the type of customers you have – a designer studio is more likely to change address than a steel plant, and it varies with the type of data – so transactions must be updated more often than demographics.

If the task is relationship marketing in business-to-business with the objective of improving retention of the most valuable customers, more demographic, preference, attitude and transaction data will be needed than if the task is to renew subscriptions. In business-to-business transactions, demographics will cover individual and company data;

preference may include fields of interest; attitude may include satisfaction ratings, propensity to buy and to recommend; transaction history would cover type and value of products or services purchased and dates. The challenge is to collect and maintain only the essential information that can be used to describe the customers' experience with the brand and to support customer loyalty objectives.

Increasing the retention of your most valuable customers requires a significant investment in CIM, but the pay-off is high. A five percentage points increase in retention rate can have an impact of anywhere between 35 and 95 per cent on customers' net present value, depending on the industry you are in, according Frederick Reichheld.

To be truly effective relationship marketing therefore requires two practices, CRM and CIM. Both are needed to deliver the desired customer experiences and to measure the impact on customers and on the bottom line.

What about your people?

Moving to relationship marketing on the Web is a change that requires a multidimensional approach. As with the management of any change, issues must be simultaneously addressed in four domains: systems, information, processes and people. Management of change is like an iceberg (see Figure 2.2) where the visible tip is the systems domain.

The mistake that is often made is to believe that change occurs when new systems and technologies are introduced and to ignore the domains below the surface. In fact, the real challenges are transforming people's motivations, redesigning processes and gathering and managing information. Take the example of a customer service organisation where 'telephone tag' is a typical occurrence. The customer is asked to call another number because the problem described is not the

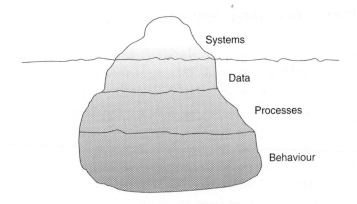

Systems

Data

Processes

Behaviour

Figure 2.2: The management of change iceberg

kind that the contacted service engineer knows how to fix. The customer has no choice but to start all over again and explain one more time the nature of the problem to a new engineer. That often happens because the behaviour of the service engineer is driven by a performance measurement system that is internally focused: productivity, turnaround time and the like. In a customer-centric organisation, the engineer would have ownership of the problem and would feel empowered to find a solution even if it were not within their competence. That is because the motivations are different, with at their base different values and different performance measures. In a customer-centric organisation the engineer would record the customer issue and transfer the record with the customer ID and the customer call to a competent colleague, who would open up the customer file, resolve the issue and close the transaction back to the originating engineer.

Web-based technology and customer information management can certainly enable the entire process and make it look seamless, but the real cause of a satisfactory outcome for the customer is the engineer's motivation.

Short-term or long-term goals?

Perhaps now is the time to revisit your expectations about being on the Web. We made the case that being on the Web is about doing relationship marketing which, in turn, is about being customer centric. If your goal is to make the transition from being a product-centric company to becoming a customer-centric one, you will have to work on all four aspects of change: people, processes, information and Web-based systems and solutions. This is not a trivial task, it takes time and significant investment, yet you cannot wait until everything is in place to show some results. You need long-term and short-term goals. You need a long-term strategy to achieve the transition and some quick wins to demonstrate the viability of the approach.

Here is a suggestion. Invite some of your key customers to define their buying process, ask them to describe their desired experiences at every major step and compare them against what they are actually experiencing now. Then ask them to prioritise the changes they would like to see in terms of value to them.

Next, assess the changes in terms of cost and impact on your company. Some may address systemic issues that cannot be resolved without some extensive process re-engineering, but some may offer the potential for quick resolution. Start from the latter and pick the one or two that have higher value from the customers' viewpoint and lower cost for you.

For example, let's say that during the pre-sale phase of the buying cycle your customers have difficulty finding adequate information about your products and services. Your sales channel is too busy and does not answer customers' enquiries promptly. This causes dissatisfaction and may lead to your losing new business. Your web site can be designed to provide the desired information including tables, menu-driven choices or configuration tools so that customers can make comparisons, narrow down their choices and make a selection. Personalisation features can also be made available to your most valuable customers to allow them, for example, to forward their enquiries by e-mail to a central marketing staff who can help them finalise the purchase decision and place the order. In this example, web site design and personalisation features can provide a quick win on two counts: delivering the desired customer experience and improving the productivity of the sales channel.

Should you go for long-term or short-term goals when you move to relationship marketing on the Web? The answer is: go for both.

From customer focus to e-CRM

Most web sites today offer information to anybody: whoever visits the site finds the same information as everybody else. The typical web site does not differentiate between prospects, first-time customers and repeat customers. The prospect is treated like a first-time customer and, what is worse, the repeat customer is treated like a prospect. The web site does not understand who the current visitor is and consequently offers the same to everybody. This works as long as individual prospects or customers have the same needs as everyone else visiting the site, which of course isn't the case.

This type of approach is mass marketing thinking that ignores the reality of today's customers. How many people have the same needs and want to see the same information displayed in the web site? Prospects have different needs to customers; repeat customers have different needs to first-time buyers, and individual repeat customers have different needs to other individual repeat customers.

Personalised information and services

If you enter a shop for the first time you may expect to be asked if you need any help. If you have purchased goods in the same shop several times in the past, when you enter the shop again, you expect the shop people to know you, to know what you have purchased in the past and to know what you like and don't like. You don't expect them to ask you the same questions all over again. You expect them to remember your previous answers. If you returned a product because of a problem, the next time you enter the shop you expect the people to know what the problem was and if the problem is solved or not.

Whatever media or channel you use to communicate with your customers (personal contact, phone, e-mail, web, WAP, paper mail, fax etc.), your customers' expectations will always be of the following sort: 'My vendor knows me, understands my problems and needs, helps me in doing my job or in improving the quality of my life *and* does not waste my time.' These expectations about a personalised experience do not depend on the media used to communicate and interact with your customers; they remain the same throughout the customer lifetime. Fulfilling these expectations is at the heart of successful customer relationship management and one-to-one marketing.

Consequently, the personalised web site we describe is a CRM web site that leverages the power and flexibility that web technology offers. Individual customers can be treated differently: they are entitled to and can see specific information, get specific services and tell you specific things about themselves. At a minimum level, by 'specific' here we mean specific with regard to who the customers are, what they purchased from you in the past and what their fields of interest are. Another aspect of specificity lies in your internal company view: different departments want and can provide different information and services to the same customers, and each department is entitled to and can provide its customers with the information and services the customers request and the department thinks are appropriate. What is important, as we said before, is that there is an internal agreement about the total customer experience to be delivered through all customer contact points.

> **KEY CONCEPT**
>
> A CRM web site provides individual customers with the right information and the right service according to their expectations and needs.

Web-enabled customer relationships

Earlier we discussed how relationship marketing is truly customer centric and how the total customer experience with your product or brand can be improved through the intelligent use of customer information. The practice of acquiring and managing customer information, or CIM, is fundamental to customer relationship management. Obviously, the stronger the relationship between you and your customers, the higher the probability that customers will provide the necessary information and tell you more about their environment and their needs.

However, going for CRM does not mean instantly gaining deep relationships with all customers. Not every customer wants to have a strong relationship with a vendor – and that's all right. No company should expect all of its customers to want strong relationships. But it is important to note that customers who are willing to build a relationship with their vendors are more likely to be or to become loyal customers, where loyalty is measured not only by their propensity to buy and to recommend, but also by their repeat purchase behaviour. So, stating 'We now have a Web-enabled CRM process' does not mean 'We now have strong relationships with our customers'. Building up a relationship over the Web takes time. As we will discuss later, you should keep this fact in mind throughout the CRM project and reflect it in your expectations.

The relationship between a customer and a vendor starts with the first contact, lasts throughout the customer lifetime and ends when the customer decides to end it, or when the vendor decides not to serve the customer any more. Therefore, a CRM web site should help the business establish and improve the relationship with the customer in every phase the customer goes through: from the first contact until the customer opts out.

A CRM web site should not focus only on one specific point of contact or one specific situation for the customer (such as a purchase or service request). It should assist the customer from the first point of contact to the next point of contact, to the next and so on. For every point of contact in the total customer experience cycle (see Figure 1.2), the CRM web site should offer appropriate personalised information, services or other benefits. Having learned what the customer wants, the web site should guide and assist the customer through the entire customer experience.

> **KEY CONCEPT**
>
> A CRM web site enables customers and businesses to build and maintain dynamic relationships with one other. It respects the relationship level chosen by the customer and is an active and intelligent interface between the customer and the vendor throughout the customer lifetime. It assists and guides the customer around the points of contact and offers value-added benefits at every step.

Competing for a scarce customer resource: time

When introducing a CRM web site, companies should be aware of entering a highly competitive environment. In the e-economy, your customers are your competitors' prospects and, possibly, customers without you being aware of it. In the bricks-and-mortar economy you may be able to monitor competitors' sales reps' visits to your accounts' premises. In the e-economy you cannot monitor your accounts' visits to your competitors' CRM web sites.

You not only compete on the sale of products and services, now you compete for your customers' attention, you compete for their interest in visiting your web site and, most of all, you compete for their time. Customers (both business and consumer) only have a limited amount of time that they are willing to spend on the Web. If your competitors offer a more attractive web site, a more compelling story and more interesting, relevant and up-to-date content, your customers may wind up spending more time on your competitors' site than on yours. Customers can and do switch to other vendors.

Therefore, companies find themselves in a new competitive context. While questions in traditional mass marketing/advertising thinking are 'Which are the best web properties to place my ad in?' or 'How often and when should my banner ad appear until they click through to my site?', the questions in the CRM web site context are quite different: 'How can I motivate my customers to spend more time on my web site? How can I motivate my customers to tell me more about themselves? How can I outperform my competitors by introducing a best-in-class CRM web site?'

If your competition is already ahead of you and uses the web and other electronic media in their CRM approach, you need to find a way to leapfrog them. Building another me-too web site is not enough in the e-world. If you plan to launch a CRM web site that just meets your competitor's current features, when it goes online it could already be too late: your competition are likely to have improved their site by that time, leaving you behind again.

To deal with this challenge you should use your one key competitive advantage: your current customers. They are your customers, after all; they know you (strengths and weaknesses), they purchased from you, they have a history with you and you know them. Their history with you is unique and you can gain a competitive advantage from it. Let the customers know and experience how you intend to continue and improve your relationship with them through modern web technology. Base your CRM web site concept on improving existing relationships with existing customers rather than on acquiring new customers. This makes sense from the profit and the competitive angle: as we said before, winning business from a new customer is five to seven times more expensive than from an existing one, while improving customer relationships through better service raises the barrier to entry to competition.

This is why we will often emphasise in this book that many major benefits for your customers come from the integration of the front-office and the back-office processes. Your web site should not only provide a smart interface for your customers' experience, but should also be linked with your internal databases, systems, processes and people. This cannot be matched by your competition. It is only you who have the history and knowledge of your customers in your back-end processes.

> **KEY CONCEPT**
>
> Your CRM web site, through its content, services and user interface, competes for your customers' attention, interest and, above all, time. Design your site around what you know about your customers in order to have them spend more of their time with you, tell you more about themselves, repurchase from you and recommend you.

In the following chapters we will highlight the relevant factors that will enable you and your company to win in this game. We will present concepts that will benefit both your customers and your company and that can be realistically implemented.

GETTING STARTED: applying one-to-one concepts to e-CRM

Five principles of e-CRM

In Chapter 1 we mentioned the one-to-one marketing approach and the challenges faced by e-marketers in implementing it. The question we would like to answer here is: 'How can the Web and related e-technologies help a company apply one-to-one concepts in an e-CRM environment?'

In *The One-to-One Fieldbook*, Don Peppers and Martha Rogers identify four implementation steps in one-to-one marketing: identify, differentiate, interact and customise. Conceptually these steps could also be applied in an e-CRM environment. However, an e-CRM environment can consist of many different components handling different customer contact points, such as a CRM web site, an e-mail marketing engine, a call centre and others. Therefore an e-CRM environment that applies one-to-one concepts and satisfies customer needs at every contact point should meet requirements that are specific to its component parts. We find it useful to test such an e-CRM environment against the following five principles:

■ As soon as a customer interacts with one of the e-CRM components, the e-CRM environment identifies them as a unique, individual customer.

■ The e-CRM environment knows how to differentiate an individual customer from all other customers – it uses customer profile data.

■ The e-CRM environment makes it easy for customers to establish contact with the enterprise and enables meaningful one-way and two-way communication through any customer-preferred media.

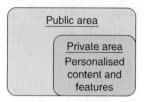

Figure 2.3: The private area offers content and features that are not accessible by the public but by individual customers only

- In the e-CRM environment customers find content and services that satisfy their individual needs and interests.
- Through the e-CRM environment the enterprise gains new knowledge about customers' needs and interests and continuously improves content and programming.

The answer to the earlier question is that the Web can indeed help your company implement one-to-one e-marketing through an e-CRM environment that satisfies the five principles outlined above.

The private area

Figure 2.3 shows the basic design adopted by most CRM-oriented web sites. In your web site you offer a public area that is accessible to anyone: there are no restrictions and anybody connected to the World Wide Web has access to it. Within your site you implement a restricted area that we call the 'private area'. Only customers with a personal unique user ID and password have access to the private area. Inside the private area your customers find personalised content and features meeting their individual needs and interests. One of the focal points in the rest of this book is how to best set up the private area for your customers and your company.

You may have heard talk about portals. Why do we choose to call the private area that and not a portal? First, there is no clear and common definition of what a portal is. Depending on whom you talk to and which software vendor you are dealing with, you will find different opinions about the scope and features of a portal. It is our view that the function of a portal is to offer personalised access to a selection of publicly available content and features. The delivery mechanism is advanced in the sense that the user can configure their own portal page up to a certain level. The type of content could include user-specified topics such as the weather forecast for a specific area, stock quotes for a specific portfolio or news items from selected categories. However, the content itself is in the public domain, it is available to anybody.

With this in mind, we also need to mark the difference between 'personalised access' and 'personalised information'. Personalised access, as we have seen above, can lead the user to dynamically configured public domain information, but it is also a prerequisite for accessing personalised information.

By introducing the expression private area we are trying to emphasise that the focus is on personalised, customised information that is not available to the public, but is applicable to one individual customer or a group of customers only. Nobody else has access to this information. With this in mind, let us focus on the information and on the personalised services that can be delivered and enabled through the private area.

Incidentally, you can assume that your competition regularly checks what services you offer on your public web site. As soon as you introduce a private area and offer personalised services there, your competition will have a harder time finding out what your services are. Even if through subterfuge your competition gains access to the private area, by becoming a customer or by collaborating with a customer that has access to the private area, this does not mean that they will know all you actually offer, because the services to which they may gain access are not the same as those you offer to the other customers.

The personalised web site

CHAPTER 3

Overview

This chapter deals with:

- Key characteristics of a personalised web site.
- The main values that a personalised web site can deliver to both the customer and the company.
- Underlying principles for building successful e-CRM web sites.

Registration

The prerequisite for any personalised user interface, content or features is that you know who is currently visiting your web site. Personalisation is only possible if you can recognise returning individual visitors, meaning that you can identify those who visit your private area on the Web.

A CRM web site recognises returning web site visitors and identifies them as individual customers.

Cookies or explicit registration and login?

While cookies are a method commonly used to recognise returning visitors, we will not dwell on the technique because it is amply described in many books and articles and because the personalisation level allowed by cookies is, in our view, insufficient. Cookies have the image of surreptitious devices, do not inspire confidence and are the subject of privacy complaints. A cookie is installed on the user's PC by the Web server passing it to the browser, unless the user has turned off the cookie capability in their browser. When the user visits a web site, the cookie is read and the PC is identified as a returning user/PC. So, the cookie does not identify a visitor but a PC. If somebody else uses the same PC, the web site cannot differentiate between the users.

We recommend establishing an explicit registration process that a customer goes through in order to gain access to the private area. After a successful initial registration and on coming back to the private area, the visitor follows a login procedure that identifies them as a unique individual (see Figure 3.1). Registration is a 'first-time and once-only' procedure through which visitors go to identify themselves in order to gain access to the private area. Login is the repetitive procedure through which visitors go each time they visit the web site and want to access the private area.

> **KEY CONCEPT**
>
> Only explicit registration for a private area can give the appropriate security.

Self-registration: how to motivate your customers to register

Many companies place a register button or link on their homepage. After clicking on 'register', the visitor is immediately asked to enter name, e-mail address, age etc. You may agree that these companies have missed the point about

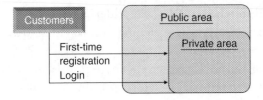

Figure 3.1: Customers need to register to access the private area and log in whenever they want to use the personalised features and content

motivating visitors to register? How many visitors will, in fact, go back to the home page or leave the site without registering? How many will register but enter wrong data, say, with regard to their age?

In order to motivate customers to register, you have to overcome some inhibitors that are in your customers' way. On the following pages we list the success principles that overcome the inhibitors and encourage your target customers to register and give you correct data.

Success principle 1: openly invite customers

Welcome your visitors and invite them to register – as simple as that! Imagine you are looking for a restaurant and you are walking down a street with several restaurants. All of them offer food and prices you like. Which one do you choose? One of the deciding factors is the feeling that you get, while observing from the outside, that inside the restaurant is welcoming and offers good service. The challenge for these restaurants is to convince you to come in when you have not yet experienced their great food and service.

When your customers are visiting your site and you want them to register, welcome them and communicate your interest. Tell your customers you want to serve them better and invite them to sample your customised services.

Let your welcome match your target groups' profile: typically, young people will respond to a welcome statement or picture differently to the way older people will. The main challenge is to design the welcome in a way that attracts your target group.

The main purpose of such an invitation is to make customers feel comfortable. Here you do not talk about the benefits yet, you do not explain why customers should register and you do not specify tangible benefits. You address their feelings: they must feel that you are interested in them and that you want to serve them well.

Where do you place the welcome? This depends on the layout of your web site – but make sure it is visible to your target group. Do not hide it, position it as a highlight.

Success principle 2: explain the benefits

You know what you offer to your customers in your private area – but your customers probably do not. It is clear for you why customers should register, but is it also clear to your customers? Think about registration like selling a product: you design the product, but to sell it you have to convince your customers.

Attract customers by explaining why. Why should they register? What do you offer them? What is the difference between the private area and the public area of your web site? What will customers get once they have registered?

Explaining the benefits not only attracts visitors, it also addresses the fears some people have. During registration they give you data about themselves. Afterwards you know them, you know their name, their e-mail address etc. – could you become a kind of Big Brother watching them? Explain the benefits to overcome that fear. Make clear why you ask them to register.

Restaurants display their menu outside, next to the entrance. People can read the menus and decide if they like what the restaurants offer. In a similar way, explain the benefits before you start asking for customer data. Select the most interesting and most relevant benefits – again, matching your target group's thinking, attitude and preferences. But do not offer benefits that you cannot deliver afterwards. Your customers will be disappointed and will not return to your site.

You may think that if you offer benefits your customers are not interested in they will not register. You may be right. Nevertheless, it is better to serve fewer customers in the private area and deliver the right services than attempt to address many customers with services that cannot be delivered properly.

Restaurant owners like customers to come in, sit down, choose from the menu, order, eat, pay and leave. They do not like people to come in, sit down, check the menu and then leave the restaurant. This would fill up their restaurants without earning revenues, and it would give a bad impression to the other guests.

You do not gain any value out of visitors who register for your site, then find out that the site does not meet their needs and never come back again. You would wind up having many visitors registered in your database without any value for you. And it would cost you money: they take disk space and, depending on the web software vendor, you would have to pay licence fees for them. In addition, there is a significant business downside: visitors who register and do not come back are disappointed visitors. Some will tell others that your site is worthless. News travel fast and wide through the Internet.

As we will discuss later in this book, the raw number of registered people is not a good measure. The number of returning visitors is a much better measure, in the same way that time spent on your site is better than eyeballs (the number of people who

KEY CONCEPT

Do not try to get everybody in your private area. Address your target group.

view your site) or clickthroughs (the number of people who arrive at your site after clicking on a banner ad).

Another good way of explaining the benefits of the private area is to offer a demonstration. When running a demonstration the customer gets a clear impression of what they get after registration without having to enter their own data right away. In most cases it is quite easy to put together a demonstration: you just set up a demo user (be sure you do not publish any confidential data to this user) and display the user ID and password. If specific and important benefits cannot be covered in the demo, explain them separately.

You might consider this step of the registration process as stating the bargain: 'In the private area of my web site I will give you benefit A and benefit B. To get these benefits, you have to register.'

If you do a good job in positioning the benefits, your customers at this point will be curious about your private area or even eager to register.

Success principle 3: display a privacy statement

There is another fear that web site visitors have when they are asked to enter data: what do you do with their data? How will you use it? Will you sell their e-mail address so they get spammed (sent junk e-mail)?

A clear privacy statement is very important to explain what you will do with visitors' data and what you will not do with it. The privacy statement will assure your visitors that you will not use their data in a way they do not like.

Examples of what you would say about the use of customer data: how you will store it; how you will improve the online experience; how you will provide and improve content and features that match customer needs and interest; how you will tailor the communication; how you will share the data only within your company.

Examples of what you would say about not using customer data: that you will not sell or rent it to external companies; that you will not use the e-mail address to run promotions unless authorised by the customer to do so.

If you intend to use customer data for specific, legally and ethically valid reasons, you must ask for the customer's permission by including an appropriate check box in the profile questionnaire. We will cover this later in this chapter.

The common understanding when entering a restaurant is that the restaurant will not sell your name and address to a food delivery service. This should also be the common understanding among companies dealing on the Web. There are different sources covering more detailed information on private issues: for US-focused sites you could check www.iab.net, the Internet Advertising Bureau (IAB), or www.the-dma.org, The Direct Marketing Association (DMA). For multi-country, internationally oriented web sites you might visit www.oecd.org, the Organisation for Economic Co-operation and Development (OECD) with participation from Europe, US, Asia and Australia. In addition to links to country governmental sites, there you will find a privacy policy statement generator that guides you through a comprehensive process for creating your own statement that you can download at the end of the process. It is not only this document that adds the value – it is the questions you are asked that you could use as a checklist.

Please be aware that countries can have their own rules, so before finalising your privacy guidelines (and back-end processes), we recommend that you check if they apply to the local laws of those countries you want to serve.

The privacy statement should be presented as clearly as the benefits of registering. A button or link to the privacy statement is fine as long as the button is visible and easily accessible.

The main purpose of the privacy statement is to build trust. If your visitors trust you they will give you data about themselves. If they do not know how you will deal with their data, the chance is high that they will not register or, worse, give you incorrect data. If your competition does not display a privacy statement, your site will differentiated. We will cover more details about privacy in Chapter 7.

Success element 4: explain the registration procedure

Your customers feel treated well, they understand what registration is for and how you will use their data. Have you done enough? No – one little step has been left out: explaining how registration works. This is not difficult but it is very important, especially for those who are not Internet savvy. Quickly explain how registration works, what fields to fill in and even what button to click if it is not fully obvious. A short description is fine.

Internet-savvy people will see no disadvantage in this explanation and newcomers will consider it a help. The only result is a positive impact on the number of registered users.

Success element 5: thanks!

Once your visitors are successfully registered, thank them for doing so. When you enter a restaurant and open the menu, many menus do not start with the food but thank the guests for having chosen the restaurant. When you purchase a car or good chocolate, you will find a thank-you note. The main purpose is to reassure customers that they have made the right choice.

Thank customers for their interest and their reliance on you. Say you are happy to serve them and that it's great to see them in the private area.

> Benefits for your customers:
>
> - Your customers feel confident and safe to register.
> - Your customers understand what they get after registration.
> - After registration your customers receive the benefits you offer them.
>
> Benefits for your enterprise:
>
> - The number of visitors who register and qualify for your target group increases.

Pre-registration

There is one weakness in the registration process described above. If you give the visitor full control on the data to enter (salutation, name, address, user ID etc.), how can you be sure that the visitor enters correct data? What if Mr Miller enters 'Mrs Smith' as the name and 'female' as the gender? The self-registration process presented above cannot prevent wrong data from being entered by your visitors. The visitor decides and if Mr Miller registers himself as a female visitor, it is up to him. If your web site differs between genders, then Mr Miller will see information and/or features designed for female visitors.

What if you need assurance that Mrs Smith really is Mrs Smith? You need this assurance particularly if you serve business customers and intend to provide contract or net pricing information to a Mrs Smith who is the purchasing manager of the company you serve. What if you decide to provide specific services only to pre-defined customers in the private area and not to others? Then you should not give full

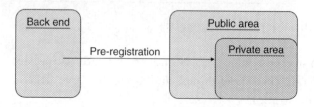

Figure 3.2: Pre-registration ensures a convenient registration process for the customer, higher security and easier back-end integration

registration control to your web site visitors: you should pre-register your customers (see Figure 3.2).

First, select the customers you want to serve in your private area, then pre-register them (meaning that *you* create a user ID and password for them) in the private area. Inform customers of their user ID and password and what they will get in the private area by letter, e-mail or phone. For example:

Dear Mrs Smith
We are happy to introduce a new service for our valued customers: within our web site we have now established a restricted area accessible only to selected customers where we offer <benefits>. To make it as easy as possible for you to benefit from this new service, we have already pre-registered you. Please visit us under the following URL <. . .> and use your personalised user ID and password, given below. After your first login you may want to change your password to retain control and privacy over access to the restricted area.

If your customers are interested in the services offered by the private area, they are likely to follow the login procedure you present.

This approach is valid for both consumers and business customers. Whether your private area is restricted to your top 20 customers or you plan to give access to one million consumers, pre-registration works the same, only the procedure will be different.

Let's assume that in your existing back-end customer database each individual customer is linked to a unique personal identification number. Extract the customers you want to serve in the private area, automatically create a user ID and password for each of them and set them up in the CRM web application. Design your CRM web application so that the customer can change the pre-assigned password and even the user ID, as long as it remains unique. It is mandatory, in order to maintain synchronisation with your customer database, to link the user ID to a unique personal identification number.

If you want to pre-register one million consumers (and do not have any further segmentation in your CRM web application), whom do you start with? The pragmatic way would be to start with those who have an e-mail address because (a) you can easily inform them about the Private Area, (b) they are likely to have access to the Internet and (c) you can see the results quickly.

Benefits for your customers:

- The effort to register is small. When they login they are already pre-registered and it is a smooth, easy process.

Benefits for your enterprise:

- You are reasonably sure that when a user named 'Mrs Smith' logs in, it is indeed Mrs Smith (unless Mrs Smith has given her user ID and password to somebody else).

CONTINUED . . .

- You can present this process as a convenient form of added value to your customers. They will feel and experience individual treatment.
- You provide controlled access to the private area to preferred customers or other named individuals that you want to reward with specific benefits as part of a loyalty scheme.

Earlier we discussed the success elements for registration (welcome, benefits, privacy statement, registration procedure and thanks). These apply equally to pre-registration. Be sure to present them to your targeted private area customers in your invitation letter or e-mail.

Identify and personalise: customer database synchronisation

Recognising a web site visitor as a customer means more than merely identifying the name. In business-to-business it also means identifying the work environment (such as company, department, site, country), the language spoken (could be different from the country language), the customer role, job title and responsibilities and so on. We will cover this topic more extensively in the next section, where we will also discuss how to motivate customers to enter their own profile data.

In addition to customer-viewable and changeable profile data, you might want to work on profile data that is not visible to the customer − the so-called hidden profile. For example, you might classify certain business customers as 'decision makers', 'specifiers' or 'influencers'. Your sales reps, not customers, would provide this type of classification. When you pre-register a customer it is up to you to feed

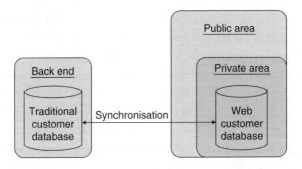

Figure 3.3: Customer database synchronisation between web front-end and back-end systems is necessary to identify and select customers for private area services

'hidden profile' data into the CRM web application. Depending on the business rules (to be discussed later) and the hidden profile, the web application can provide different information to different individuals.

All of the above can be turned into significant customer benefits and a competitive advantage for you through a very important process: the synchronisation between the web customer database and your internal, traditional customer database.

Suppose that through your CRM web site, you want to run an up-sell promotion only to customers who purchased a specific product from you two years ago. What does it take to identify the target customers?

Synchronisation between your traditional customer database (built over the years in your company) and your web customer database (containing all registered customers and their profile data) is one of the key success factors of the overall e-CRM concept (see Figure 3.3).

Let's assume that your company has an internal (traditional) back-end customer database. All customers who purchased from you in the past are stored in the internal database. Let's also assume that some of them have individually registered in the private area. The goal is to link all of the known attributes and data, wherever they are stored, to individual customers so that an appropriate customer selection can be executed. The process is to match every customer who registered in the private area periodically with the corresponding customer data stored in the internal customer database. That is in short what we mean by database synchronisation, so that you can identify the individual customers registered in the web customer database as your current customers.

Another advantage of synchronisation is that you can easily update your traditional database with data that your customers have entered or changed in the private area. So if, for example, your customers change their address online, they can also be changed automatically in the internal customer database, which improves the quality of your customer database.

By going for both pre-registration and customer database synchronisation, you have an opportunity to specify the unique customer ID that will be used to synchronise the web customer database and your traditional customer database.

However, the identification process is often quite cumbersome to perform, particularly the first time (most likely a semi-automatic or manual process). Nevertheless, the advantages to be gained are enormous. Why? Because as soon as you have performed successfully the 'Who's who' in your databases, you can address your target customers through your CRM web application and you can, therefore, apply one-to-one marketing on the Web. The procedure is illustrated in Figure 3.4.

First, define the target group for the campaign, customer event or other marketing activity and run a selection in your traditional customer database. Then in the CRM activity parameters, specify the messages to be provided to selected customers, when the campaign should start and any other parameters. Your CRM web application takes both the

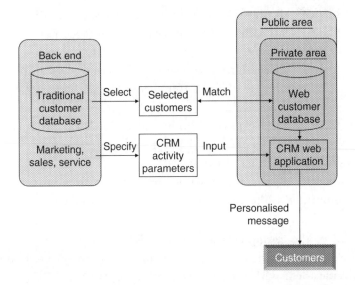

Figure 3.4: The combination of customer database synchronisation and the private area allows marketing, sales and support to deliver highly flexible and personalised campaigns

selected customers list and the CRM activity parameters as input. As soon as the selected customers log in to the private area, the CRM web application provides them with personalised messages.

Below are examples of how marketing, sales, service and support departments could use the e-CRM environment, provided that the information needed to select customers is stored and maintained in the traditional customer database through the practice of customer information management:

- Identify all customers who purchased product XYZ three years ago. I'd like to run an upgrade campaign to increase revenues.
- Identify all customers who had a problem with our products during the past three months. I'd like to check if they were satisfied with customer service.

- Identify all first-time buyers in the past three months. I'd like to send a thank-you message to reinforce their decision to buy.
- Identify all customers whose support contracts expire next month. I'd like to offer a contract upgrade with automatic renewal.
- Identify all customers who attended the XYZ product introductory seminar. I'd like to promote our new advanced seminar to them.
- Identify all customers whose warranty expires next month. I'd like to propose a support contract to them.

In all of the examples above your CRM web site could address exactly those customers who have been selected and provide them with a customised message, such as:

Dear Mrs Smith

You attended the introductory seminar <title>. We have now launched our new advanced follow-up seminar <title2>. For further information, please check . . .

Through the power and flexibility offered by the implementation of this concept on the Web, multiple campaigns are possible at the same time without significant incremental cost. By contrast, if you ran traditional mailing campaigns, you would often find it too costly and logistically difficult to execute multiple campaigns at the same time.

 Vital questions and answers: Private Area and Database synchronisation

When going for database synchronisation you will meet several challenges:

CONTINUED . . . **Vital questions and answers:**
Private Area and Database synchronisation

Database synchronisation is a cumbersome job

- Accept the effort, the gain is vastly superior to the pain.
- If possible, pre-register your customers to have the opportunity to specify a common identifier to synchronise the traditional and the web customer databases.

If your company runs multiple customer databases, the customer identifier has to be unique among all databases

- reach an agreement among the departments involved, start with the most important database, and then expand to the other databases step by step.

Timing, priorities and approval

- If multiple departments join the CRM project, you will have to decide on timing (how often a customer should be provided with a personalised message), priorities (what message the customer should see first) and approval processes (who is allowed to provide specific messages to specific customers).
- Establish a CRM work group that deals with this type of question. The work group should have representatives from all departments involved in the CRM project.

Misuse of the private area concept could decrease the performance of your CRM site and confuse your customers through a high number of personalised messages and content items

- Plan, do, check and act. Take a quality approach.

CONTINUED ... **Vital questions and answers:**
Private Area and Database synchronisation

◆ Define the amount of personalisation, i.e. the number of personalised content items at the beginning and select and plan your software and hardware accordingly.

◆ When the CRM web application is up and running, observe performance, ask your customers how they experience this new service and improve according to their input.

Benefits for your customers:

● They receive in-time, personalised and relevant messages.

Benefits for your enterprise:

● Once the process is set up, it takes only a short time to address targeted individuals one-to-one.
● Multiple departments can benefit from the concept: marketing, sales, service, in fact all customer-facing departments can provide customised messages.
● You can effectively execute one-to-one marketing.
● Costs per campaign are low, the ROI per campaign increases. The number of campaigns can increase.

Profiling

While registration (be it self-registration or pre-registration) enables the CRM environment to *identify* individual

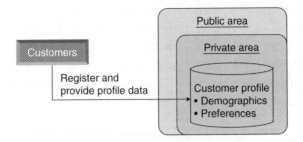

Figure 3.5: Obtaining the right customer profile data is an art on its own. High-quality customer data allows the enterprise to provide better customer service

customers, their profile enables you to *differentiate* your customers. A customer profile is a set of data describing attributes specific to the individual customer.

Why profiling? What is it important for? It is the prerequisite for personalisation. Whenever you intend to personalise the customer experience in your web site, an e-mail newsletter or any other service, you must first know what customers prefer to receive, how to greet them, how to communicate with them. In this chapter we concentrate on how to motivate customers to tell you as much as possible about themselves, thereby releasing their profile data to you.

We must distinguish between demographic data and preferences (see Figure 3.5). Examples of demographic data are name, address, phone number, age, gender. Examples of customer preferences are receive promotional information yes/no, credit card preferences, car rental preferences etc.

Let's suppose you have invited and motivated a customer to go through the registration process. Now you have the opportunity to obtain the data you want from the customer. You may believe that good marketers have to get as much data as possible from their customers. It is very easy to provide a questionnaire with dozens of questions – but it is also very easy for the customer to leave your site unnerved by all those questions taking up their time or, worse, asking for very personal data. The result could be that fewer customers subscribe to your service or that those who do give you the wrong data.

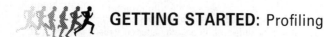 **GETTING STARTED:** Profiling

Following is a list of recommendations on how to set up a professional profiling process with the following main objective: targeted customers filling in complete and accurate profiling data.

Focus on what you really need to know

Work on the list of all the information you want to obtain from your customers – prioritise and only ask for information needed for the task of supplying the desired service. Of course, it is very interesting to know a lot about your customers. But in the e-CRM world, it is not the quantity of data that counts, but the quality. As we said before, data is a perishable commodity and it costs money to keep it up to date. Often companies ask for data like age, marital status or number of children without the objective of serving the customer better using this data. If you do not plan to customise your services differently based on age, do not ask for age. Only ask for data that you need in order to serve the customer better.

The positive effect of this recommendation is manifold: you have a clear focus on the task, you have less data to store and maintain, the questionnaire your customer has to fill in is smaller and your customer won't be irritated by the questionnaire.

Explain what you need the data for

Tell your customers what you will do with the data and how you will use it to improve their online (or offline) experience. If customers understand and appreciate what you will do with their data, they will release it. If they do not understand, either they will not enter the data or they will enter incorrect data. Very often people are asked for their age. If you cannot or if you do not explain to your customers why you ask for their age, why should the customer fill in that part of the questionnaire? If you can explain to the customer why you need the information and how you will use it to their benefit, they are more likely to be agreeable to releasing the information.

Show the progress of the profiling process

(This only applies to lengthy forms.) Even after limiting the number of questions to the most important ones, your registration form may appear to be lengthy. In this case divide the form into several consecutive forms (steps) and on top of each form display what step the customer is in, e.g. Step 3 of 4. In this way the customer is always informed of the progress made and how much is still left to do and, hopefully, will remain motivated to complete the registration process.

Offer a short cut

Do not force customers to complete the entire profiling process. Customers are not always interested in working their way through a lengthy profile form. Offer the option to stop the profiling, save the work done so far and come back to the profile when it is convenient to the customer. If the customer has not answered all the questions, set a default where appropriate or design your applications so they do not have to work with the empty data until the customer has completed it. If you set defaults, make sure you don't set them the way *you* want them to be set, but as your customers would like them to be set or as the legal restrictions allow them to be set.

Respect customers' privacy with regard to sensitive information

Imagine again that you enter a shop and one of the first questions the shop owner asks you is the level of your income – how would you react? You would be probably startled at first and then indignant about the brazen attempt to extract such sensitive information from you. If you were the shop owner you would not ask such a question point blank, even though it would be very useful to know your customer's income. You might get that information later, perhaps indirectly, after having established a solid relationship with the customer.

Similarly, if in your registration form you ask for private or sensitive data, some of your customers might feel offended and will quit the registration process or give you wrong information. None of that helps you. We recommend that either you explain very clearly why you ask for that sort of information, or that you do not ask for it at this stage.

Relationship building takes time. If after registration it is your customers' experience that you treat their data with care in accordance with your privacy statement, that you serve them better and offer additional benefits based on the data you have, over time some of them will become motivated to release more information about themselves. Even though you would like to know your customers' income and have good reasons to ask the question now, it may be wiser to wait and ask the question later.

Pre-fill the registration form with customer data already known to you

So far we have mainly talked about data entered by customers, which we call data *from* the customers. There is

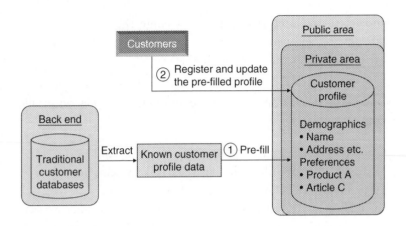

Figure 3.6: By pre-filling customer profile data, you simplify the process for customers and can use their corrections to update your databases

one other category, data *about* the customers, which may be stored within the enterprise's traditional customer databases. If you pre-register your customers, you can make the profiling process easier and more convenient for them by filling in data already known to you before you ask the customer to complete their profile (see Figure 3.6).

If you already know the customer's address or phone number, why bother to ask for this data again? Pre-fill those fields and at the same time show that you know the customer. This will make the customer feel comfortable (the vendor remembers me!) and simplifies the process (I have to enter less data). If the data you provide is not correct, it is up to the customer to overwrite it.

Make it easy for customers to update their profile

Getting customers to update their records in your web database is good CIM practice, together with database synchronisation mentioned earlier. Make it easy and clear for your customers how to change their profile in the private area and let them know that they can change their profile whenever they want. This is particularly important in an age of increasing change and mobility.

Update your back-end systems with customer-supplied profile data immediately

Once the customer has entered profile data (and perhaps changed your pre-filled fields), feed this information right away into the back-end systems that use the data. If you ask the customer to update the address field, the customer expects you to use the updated address immediately after having completed the profile. Transmit the updated address to all systems that use customer addresses, such as mailing or billing systems. If you have a traditional customer address master file, consider the data entered by the customer as the master data. If you deal with multiple addresses per customer (general address, invoice-to address, ship-to address), make it clear to the customer which address you are asking for and feed that information into your master file.

The important factor is time. If customers provide new address data today, you should use the updated address in tomorrow's mailing. If customers update their profile today to signify they no longer wish to receive paper mail, do not send them the planned direct mail shot tomorrow.

If you think, 'I can't do it this way. I must send the customer's addresses to my printer a month before the mailing goes out' – think again! The CRM environment centres on the customer, not on existing processes. When customers say they no longer want to receive paper mail, your direct mail process should react immediately. If it doesn't, it should be redesigned.

If, for whatever reason, you cannot use tomorrow the profile data entered by the customer today (depending on the business you are in, this could even be a question of minutes), there are two alternatives. Either set the right expectations when asking for the data: 'We do our best to use this address provided by you as soon as possible in all of our communications. Please give us < so many days > for doing so.' (This sounds strange in the Internet economy, doesn't it?) Or don't ask for the address yet, which means that you postpone the profile question until you can be sure of using the customer data promptly.

Evolve customers' profiles over time

If your customers see that the level of service they receive has improved based on the profile information they supplied, they will gain trust in you. After some time, perhaps a few months, you might consider asking for more profile data. For example, when a customer logs in one day, you could pop up a message asking the customer to go to the personal profile log and enter additional information. Or, more conveniently for the customer, you could ask for the new information directly in the pop-up window. This way you enrich your customer profile over time, while also improving your services and benefits for your customers.

Benefits for your customers:

- Improved service depending on how you use the information supplied by the customers.

Benefits for your enterprise:

- You gain a clear understanding about what profile data is truly important to your CRM activity.
- Your target customers register and release complete and correct information.

CONTINUED . . .

- The quality of your customer database improves as your customers update their records.
- You have an excellent base from which to offer personalised services and offers.

Let customers help themselves

Not all customers want to place calls on a call centre. There is the inevitable waiting time spent listening to odd music or to unsolicited sound bites of advertising, plus the fact that few call centres are available 24 hours a day, 7 days a week. Some customers would rather get direct access to the information they need to do their job or solve a problem whenever they need it or whenever it suits them. Help-service, also called self-service or self-help, solves two main issues for your customers: they do not have to queue when calling the call centre and they can immediately save and print the information they retrieve.

There are several widely known approaches on how to offer web help-service: a table with FAQs (frequently asked questions and their answers), a search engine that can look up keywords in a database, a list featuring the top 10 questions of the week and so on.

Whatever the approach, the challenge is to know what is of interest to customers and what they look for when using web help-service. To find this out we suggest that you do the following:

- Collect information from the call centre, regularly analyse what questions customers ask when calling the call centre or when talking to field engineers and to sales representatives, prioritise those questions and put them into the self-service application.

■ Log and analyse the key words that customers enter in the search engine. If customers have questions and use a web search feature, the keywords they enter are clear indicators of what they are looking for.

■ Check the questions customers ask at all points of contact. This is a more proactive approach. As we discussed earlier in this book, understanding the total customer experience, by analysing what happens at the different points of contact, is also an excellent way to anticipate the questions your customers will ask: Where is the retail outlet closest to me? How does 'change order' work? What payment terms do you offer? How do I use a specific feature of the product?

Benefits for your customers:

• Higher customer satisfaction because they can find the information they need when they need it.

Benefits for your enterprise:

• Fewer calls per customer. The more questions customers can find answers for themselves, the fewer customer calls to the call centre.

• More traffic on your web site, which increases the opportunity for up-selling and cross-selling.

Let customers find the information

Web sites offer a great deal of information, but it is often quite difficult for visitors to find exactly the information they are looking for. A personalised web site, on the other hand, can provide fast and convenient access to product information, articles, press releases, FAQs – whatever information customers declare an interest in. The goal is to let customers find all the information *and only* the information that is relevant and beneficial for them.

The challenge is that different customers have different information needs and personal content preferences. The objective is to offer a personalised content experience to customers: when individual customers visit the personalised web site, they find exactly and only the information they have profiled for – the information they are interested in is defined in their profile log. The information itself is built in the background by the content providers – perhaps in your company (marketing, customer service and support etc.) or contracted out – who also define the target groups (or 'tags') per content.

When a visitor enters the private area, the web application performs a match between the customer profile and the content tags. All documents whose tags match the customer profile become accessible and are made visible to the visitor. All documents whose tags do not match the customer profile remain hidden and are not shown to the visitor.

The approach discussed in Figure 3.7 is *customer driven*: customers define through their profiles the information that is delivered to them. As customisation power is handed over to customers, the challenge at the back end is to restrict the definition of target groups per content. Content creators tend to overestimate the interest that customers may have in their content; consequently, they may define many more target groups for their content than necessary, which results in content overload for the customers. The content management function discussed in Chapter 2 should make sure that only the appropriate target groups are tagged to the content items or content categories.

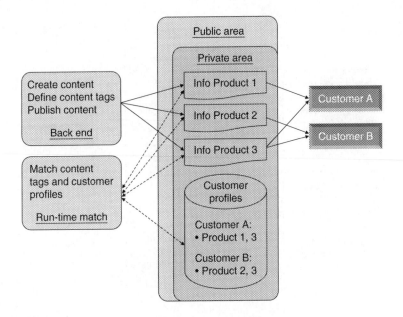

Figure 3.7: If customers find all the content and only the content relevant to them, they will come back regularly to your site

There is another approach to personalising content, which is *enterprise driven*. In this case content personalisation is based on so-called business rules. Content providers and other decision makers in your company can define the rules that determine what content is made visible and when to online visitors. Here are some examples (also see Figure 3.8):

- *Online behaviour.* Rules can be based on the current visitor's behaviour in the web site. *IF the visitor puts a specific product in the shopping basket THEN offer accessories or complementary products.*
- *Historical data in profile.* Rules can be based on the visitor's purchase history data in the profile. *IF the customer has purchased a specific product last year THEN offer an upgrade promotion. IF the customer is a gold customer*

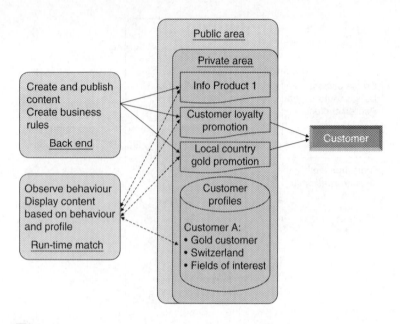

Figure 3.8: Flexible campaign personalisation is a key success factor for increased sales

THEN offer a customer loyalty promotion. IF the customer is a Gold customer AND IF the customer is interested in product <xyz> AND IF the customer is located in <country>, THEN display <country> <xyz> gold promotion.

As this approach is enterprise driven, the risk is that customers can receive information they are not interested in. Business rules should be added carefully so as not to overload customers with information they don't need and by respecting customer preferences.

The power of web site personalisation comes from two elements: content that matches customers' profiles and integration at the back end with internal customer databases.

Benefits for your customers:

- They find all the information and only information that is relevant to them.

Benefits for your enterprise:

- Increased web site traffic because customers who find personalised, relevant content keep coming back.
- The more customers trust your content, the higher is the likelihood that they will pay attention to your messages – which improves your time-to-customer.
- Personalised content is a key enabler of customer-centric marketing.

Integrate e-CRM with back-end systems

There are many touch points between the customer and the enterprise throughout the total customer experience. At every touch point the customer has a specific need that needs to be met by the enterprise. The strategy for implementing web-supported CRM (e-CRM) requires you to fulfil as many of these needs as possible by integrating the Web with your back-end systems.

One-way back-end integration

The main objective for one-way back-end integration is to deliver valuable information to customers during the sale and after-sale part of the buying process. In terms of information retrieval, here we need to distinguish between online access to the back-end infrastructure and offline access, that is, access to information copies that reside in the web environment (see Figure 3.9).

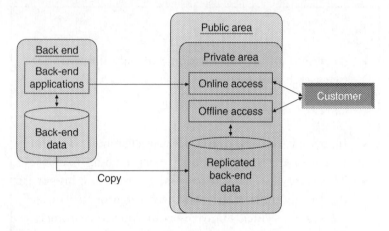

Figure 3.9: If the web front end delivers personalised data from your back-end systems to your customers, then competition is *more than* a click away

Whether you choose to go for online or offline access depends on the nature of your business and on your customer needs. An online connection from the Web to your back-end systems gives customers the benefit of access to up-to-date, real-time information. The benefits to the enterprise are a more competitive operational infrastructure, a diminished workload for the customer service department and higher customer satisfaction. There are challenges for IT, however, usually in the areas of security and high availability of your back-end systems, which may require modifications to the existing back-end infrastructure in order to meet the new model and to handle the additional load.

If it is not that critical for the customer to have immediate access to up-to-the-minute information, offline access is adequate. Offline access requires you to set up processes that periodically extract the information out of the back-end systems and replicate it in the web environment. The benefit to the customer is constant access to information, even if the back-end systems are not available for some reason. The advantage for the enterprise is less complication, with security and high availability at the back-end. The disadvantage is greater process work because an additional data structure needs to be managed and backed up, and data consistency must be assured.

Online access examples:

- Check product availability.
- Check order status (personalised information).
- Check delivery status (personalised information).
- Check open service case (personalised information).

Offline access examples:

- Look up order history (personalised information).
- Look up service case history (personalised information).
- Look up invoice history (personalised information).
- Help-service: look up knowledge base.

Two-way back-end integration

Integration with back-end systems need not be one way only. It is also possible and very effective from the CRM viewpoint to feed information from customers into the back-end systems as requested by the customer. The benefit to the customer is higher quality of service and the benefit to the enterprise is a more efficient CIM process (see Figure 3.10).

Examples:

- 'Configure my phone bill'. The customer determines how call detail lines are grouped and sorted (by date/time, call-to number, duration or price). The next invoice the customer receives is sorted and presented the way the customer likes and understands it.
- 'Change my address'. As discussed earlier, if the customer enters/updates profile data such as address or phone

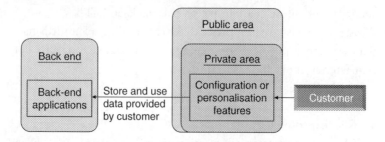

Figure 3.10: Two-way back-end integration ensures service quality and speeds up processes

number, this data should go directly to the back-end systems for future usage.

- 'Change my order': The customer can change ordered items, ship-to address or invoice-to address.

Your back-end infrastructure and data are not available to your competition. As you deliver more benefits to your customers based on back-end integration (one way or two way), it becomes more difficult for your competition to emulate you. Strong back-end integration can be a key differentiator when customers compare services offered from different suppliers.

Benefits for your customers:

- Easy and fast access to information during and following purchase.
- Control over certain personal information fields.

Benefits for your enterprise:

- Reduced workload on customer service for standard enquiries.

- Stronger competitive advantage by offering information that competition cannot duplicate.
- Improved service quality, reliability and customer satisfaction.

Personalise as many features as possible

In many web sites online shopping is an important part of the total customer experience. We will not cover here the shopping features, order status features or similar services delivered by the many applications available in the market, because a great deal of literature already exists on these features. What we discuss here is how to *personalise* these features and services to implement e-CRM more effectively. Obviously, many different scenarios could be considered and it would be impossible to describe all possible personalisation options, so we will mention just a few examples. Which personalised features you finally implement depends on the business you are in and on your customers' preferences.

 IMPLEMENTATION CHECKLIST:
Personalisation

Consumers

◆ A regular online shopper always puts certain specific items in their shopping basket among other purchases. Next time the customer goes shopping, the shopping application asks if those specific items should go into the basket. In this example, the shopping application observes the customer's shopping behaviour and customises the user interface based on the acquired learning. As not all customers appreciate this feature, the customer profile software should allow them to turn the feature on or off.

◆ Alternatively, the customer can store frequently purchased items in a shopping basked and save it. Next time the customer goes shopping, they can retrieve the shopping basket and modify its contents.

◆ The customer can configure the position of preferred features and content items in the personalised user interface. If the first action the customer always performs after logging in is to check new arrivals in a specific product category, it would be convenient for the customer to find that precise button at the top of everything else.

◆ The online shopping feature remembers payment preferences, delivery preferences and ship-to and invoice-to preferences, and offers this data as default.

Business customers

◆ If a customer is the purchasing department manager of a client firm, they are authorised to access order status information for all orders placed by the department. If, however, the customer is an employee of the purchasing department, they can only look up the order status of the orders they have placed.

◆ The same purchasing department manager from time to time requests information about individual orders, but usually asks for an order summary. The order summary is set up as the default request, so when the department manager enters the order status feature, the order summary is offered first without further clicks.

◆ Customised product catalogue 1: only display selected products agreed between the customer and your enterprise.

◆ Customised product catalogue 2: include products not available to other customers such as special configurations.

◆ Customised pricing: do not calculate list prices but net prices according to the purchase agreement between the customer and your enterprise.

◆ Contacts: if you serve a large account, it is likely that each customer in the account will have different contacts in your enterprise. A list featuring all the right contacts in your enterprise could be made available to each customer in the account.

Benefits to your customers:

● Higher personalisation results in faster access to information and higher convenience in using the site.

Benefits to your enterprise:

● The easier and more convenient it is for your customers to use your web site, the more likely it is that they will return and shop again.

● The more personalised the web environment is for the customer, the less likely it is that the competition can match it.

● As a personalised environment makes it easier for the customer to find relevant information, it decreases the number of calls for routine information and, therefore, the workload on your enterprise.

Make it easy for the customer to communicate with you

Perhaps the customer does not find the information they are looking for or they have selected a product but have a question about the right configuration, or have filled the shopping basket but do not know how to complete the order form. Whenever customers have questions while visiting a web site, it should be made easy and convenient for them to contact the enterprise through the Web.

Some basic and more advanced features that support this e-CRM requirement are listed in Table 3.1.

Benefits for your customers:

- Customers have the choice of communicating with you however they like.
- Customers are given the means to contact you any time they have a question and in whatever process they find themselves.

Benefits for your enterprise:

- Every customer contact gives the opportunity to serve the customer better and to earn their loyalty.
- Every customer contact gives you the opportunity to up-sell and cross-sell.
- Every properly handled product enquiry at the time the customer thinks about purchasing improves the chances of closing the deal.

Personalised company information

Large companies often require specific, highly customised information. If you serve a large company you can structure a private area where the customer can find company-specific information such as contract and pricing information, the

Table 3.1: Make it easy for customers to communicate with you and at the same time increase your capability for selling and serving customers

Feature	How to use	Characteristics
Web-embedded e-mail link	Customer clicks on e-mail link, standard e-mail client opens. Customer sends e-mail to address as specified in e-mail link.	Customer can use the e-mail client with which they are familiar. Low implementation effort. This feature cannot offer any customisation or advanced security.
Web form	Customer enters data into a form. Form content is sent to the enterprise's back end.	Clear guidance for the customer as to what to fill in. Customisation is possible (e.g. pre-filled with customer profile data). Web site security can be applied. Independent of customer's e-mail client.
Chat-with-me button	Customer clicks on the button and a contact centre agent opens a chat space.	Both the contact centre agent and the customer 'talk' via a chat. This is especially helpful if the customer has only one phone line that is occupied by the Internet connection.
Call-me-now button	Customer clicks on the button and receives a call from a call centre agent.	Customer receives on-time response and phone support. Customer profile data can be provided to the call centre agent via computer telephony integration.
Web collaboration	Customer uses the Call-me-now feature. In parallel to talking to the agent, the agent sees the page(s) that the customer has opened.	No need for the customer to explain where in the Web they are. Avoids misunderstandings. Several advanced features are possible: the agent can follow the customer through multiple web pages; customer and agent can share the same form; the agent can run an application demonstration.
Open case, view case	Customer enters a service request into a special form (customer opens a case) and tracks the case status to see progress.	Customer can request service without calling the service call centre. Customer has online access to status information. Improves call centre load balance.
Multi-mode feedback	Customer defines how to receive response from the call centre (or other departments): voice, e-mail, SMS, WAP, message on personalised web site.	Customer receives response through preferred channel. Usage of multiple channels reduces load on call centre agents.

right contact names in your enterprise, information about past purchases, pre-packaged product offers and planning information about forthcoming new products.

Within a large company, individual customers have different information needs depending on their job function and position in the hierarchy. If you sell IT equipment, for example, the purchasing department will need different information from you to the system analysts in the IT department. The system analysts will need different information to the chief information officer.

In principle, all this information could be sent to customers via e-mail. However, the benefits of making the information available to individual customers through a private area are significant:

- Customers can be sure that they will always have access to the most recent version. If you send e-mail with attachments, you can never be sure that your customers read the latest version. By providing the information on the Web through the private area, you have control over the recency and destination of the information.
- Your customer does not have to store and maintain information sent by e-mail, but can find all the relevant information through a specific entry point.
- E-mail is not secure. Its use may not be appropriate for sensitive information. It can be infected by viruses and it can be tampered with by hackers. If you offer a secured private area within your web site, you resolve these issues.

As we discussed before, a personalised company information service for customers requires content management, a user-friendly interface for publishing the content plus a solid commitment from the different content providers within the enterprise (customer service, sales, operations) to regularly make available up-to-date content. The content providers will be willing to collaborate if they see the benefits:

- Fewer phone calls and fewer enquiries in the in-basket for sales and service reps. This means freeing up time for selling or for critical support tasks for the reps.
- Better customer service that provides relevant information in a secure, easy-to-use environment.

Benefits for your customers:

- Fast and easy access to relevant, company-specific, private, personalised information.

Benefits for your enterprise:

- Competitive advantage and stronger customer loyalty through offering a highly customised service.
- Fewer calls from the customer, as the information is made available on the Web.
- Better protection of the information through a secure private area.

Personalisation versus performance trade-offs

As personalisation consumes system resources, any e-CRM design will be confronted with trade-offs between personalisation features and system performance. It is best to plan how to deal with the trade-offs before starting, otherwise there is a high chance of failure.

KEY CONCEPT

Personalisation is a key element of any e-CRM strategy. Trade-offs need to be made between level of personalisation to be implemented and system performance. Needs change over time. Keep current on customers' changing needs and profiles.

GETTING STARTED: Personalisation versus performance

Performance issues

A personalised web site builds the web page at the time the user logs in or clicks on specific links. It is at this moment that the web application checks the profile, retrieves the appropriate content, puts it into a sequence and offers it to the visitor. The more rules and matches are performed, the more system resources are requested. The more a web application has to personalise dynamically, the more system performance is needed. Web users no longer put up with poor performance. If they do not get fast response time, they become nervous and even leave the site – perhaps not coming back again. To avoid performance bottlenecks, the personalisation requirements should be clearly defined *before* making decisions on hardware, network and software resources.

To reduce some of the performance issues, you could decide that some of the personalisation will take place offline when the user is not working on the site. For example, customer intelligence routines could update the customer profile so that the next time the customer logs in, certain pre-defined content and features are made available. This approach requires a balance to be struck between really necessary online personalisation and system performance.

Another way to deal with system load is to queue incoming login requests. If the system hosting the web site is running at peak load level, the next visitor asking to log in receives a message that it will take 60 seconds before they are let in. If all requested logins can be prioritised based on profile data, waiting time etc., the system will not run into overload, new visitors will get a clear message to set the expectations right, and visitors currently logged in will not experience longer response times during their sessions.

ROI time horizon

Personalisation does not come for free. The closer to one-to-one you want to take personalisation, the costlier in terms of time and budget it will become. It is not uncommon to underestimate how long it takes to learn what your customers really need, to underestimate the resources needed and to overestimate ROI (return on investment) in the short-term. As previously said, relationships evolve over time and ROI expectations based on improved relationships should reflect a mid-term strategy, not a short-term one.

You can misapply personalisation

You analyse, you specify rules, you integrate – you do things right, but this does not prevent you from personalising the wrong way. The automated personalisation process builds up screens for the individual users, yet there is the danger that the customers find information, messages or features that do not meet their individual needs – or, worse, that upset them. On the road from mass marketing to mass customisation to one-to-one personalisation, the difficulty in meeting individual customer needs increases.

As you serve real people through personalisation, the question is not *if* their individual needs differ but *how* they differ. Any rule means generalisation, so the success of personalisation rules depends on the likelihood that the rules match customer needs and behaviour.

Let's say that you are in the consumer business and you have decided to apply a collaborative filtering tool for the personalisation process. Collaborative filtering is a self-learning process that makes online recommendations to a visitor by making a comparison between the visitor's purchase or content selection and what other visitors with a similar profile have selected in the past.

This means that you are making the explicit assumption that, because many similar individuals have purchased a specific item, the current visitor should also be interested in it. It is a matter of probability. If you are right, your visitor will appreciate the recommendation. If you are wrong, the customer may neglect the message or, worse, get the impression that you do not really understand their individual needs. In addition, needs change over time – if personalisation does not follow these changes in individual needs, it will fail to provide any benefit. So start by satisfying basic personalisation needs and evolve over time into more sophisticated personalisation schemes as you learn more about your customers. Regularly ask for feedback from your customers and ask them to update their profile to keep the personalisation application current with changing needs.

E-mail
marketing

CHAPTER 4

Overview

In this chapter we focus on e-mail marketing, in particular:

- Why it is one of the most flexible and efficient means of communication.
- How to develop and maintain consistent and on-going customer interest.
- How e-mail marketing in combination with traditional direct marketing can boost return on investment.

Have you ever subscribed to a newsletter and become dissatisfied with it? Have you ever let a company e-mail you and been irritated with what they sent you? If so, those companies failed in their e-mail marketing strategy, they did not meet your expectations and could not maintain your interest in what they were communicating. This is why customers often unsubscribe from e-mail services or even send complaints about how those companies waste their time when they are not taken off the distribution list quickly enough.

In Chapter 3 we showed the benefits of using the private area of a personalised web site rather than using e-mail in the context of providing a personalised customer information service. Here we will demonstrate how to develop and execute the right e-mail marketing strategy for specific objectives. A well-conceived e-mail marketing service could very well serve your customers and support your business objectives, especially if it is integrated with your back-end systems and if the e-mail marketing system works together with the private area of the personalised web site.

Objectives

E-mail is a universal communication tool. It is easy to use, it
works independently of the
users' technology platform and
it can be employed at any time.

> ### KEY CONCEPT
>
> E-mail marketing can be a very effective instrument for reaching the enterprise's business goals.

Enterprises use e-mail to communicate directly with their customers, to inform them of new developments, to create a dialogue and to maintain relationships. E-mail, like all communication tools, can be integrated in a marketing communications strategy to support broad objectives such as branding or public relations. However, it can also be utilised as the primary communication tool for a number of marketing objectives. In this case we speak of e-mail marketing.

 IMPLEMENTATION CHECKLIST: E-mail marketing

The following is a typical list of objectives that companies can pursue with e-mail marketing. Of course, based on your own situation you may have different objectives and priorities.

Increase web site traffic

Your e-mail messages should include links to your web site where your prospect and customers can find more detailed information and where they can download a specific article or find ordering information. This way your e-mail messages become a major tool for increasing traffic on your web site.

Announce new products and services

You can inform your prospects and customers about new products and services and include graphical presentations or thumbnail pictures, together with links to your web site.

Promote current products, up-sell and cross-sell

You can run targeted e-mail campaigns to selected customers for offering specific promotions. Based on customer profiles, you can promote trade-ups to higher-value products or offer complementary products and services.

Market research

You can run e-mail surveys among your customers and find out what they think about the quality of your products, services and organisation. You can ask them questions about their preferences and interests. Because of the immediacy of the medium, e-mail surveys should have a few simple questions to generate a good response.

One-to-one customisation

E-mail campaigns, as we will see later, are more flexible and more easily implemented than paper mail campaigns. You can send one-to-one messages to your customers and can therefore provide very valuable, customised information that supports your e-CRM strategy.

Lower costs and increased coverage

After having made the initial investment to design and set up a complete e-mail marketing environment, e-mail marketing campaigns cost significantly less than traditional media marketing campaigns. That is because you (a) have no printing costs – the recipient does the printing; (b) mailing costs are lower – the unit cost of an e-mail message is much lower than physical mail; and (c) you can plan and run more campaigns a year than with traditional paper mail activities – scheduling is much simpler and set-up and lead times are shorter.

Immediate response

This is also a key benefit of e-mail. Receivers of an e-mail can either immediately hit the reply-to-sender button or click on a hyperlink and be connected to your web site. On the other hand, response rates, measured in percentage of responses to an e-mail campaign, are a function of how well targeted the mailing list is and how good the offer. Average e-mail response rates are in the region of 2 per cent but good, well-targeted promotion campaigns can reach 10–15 per cent response rates or higher.

Shorter time-to-customer

It usually takes longer to design, print and send out physical direct mail than it does to design and send out e-mail. E-mail marketing gives you the advantage of shorter time-to-customer, which means that your information reaches the customer sooner and you can shorten the turnaround time of your communications. This in turn can lead to increased sales.

Track results

While testing campaigns and tracking results is possible with both traditional mail and e-mail, it is much easier with e-mail. Hyperlinks offer the capability to create logs that, as an example, let you track how many customers have read a specific article and then purchased a specific item.

Competing for customer attention

If, before setting up e-mail communications with your customers, you were to ask them for their gut-level feedback, you would probably get comments like: 'Send me only the stuff that interests me', 'Do not waste my time', 'Make it short and clear'. The bottom line for customer expectations with regard to e-mail is that they will accept e-mail only if it contains information that is relevant to them, useful and to the point.

It is not unusual for business people to receive 50 to 100 or even more e-mail messages per day. Which messages will they spend time reading? Which messages will they delete without even opening? It is only if your messages consistently deliver relevant and beneficial information that your customers will continue to read them.

By engaging in e-mail marketing you are not only in competition with other vendors' e-mail messages, you are in competition with all the e-mail messages and all the paper mail and other printed material they receive. You compete for your customers' attention, time and resources to download and print information from your web site and for their interest and willingness to follow up on your messages.

That is not a trivial task. In this chapter we hope to demonstrate how to establish a professional e-mail marketing capability that reaches the right target customers with the right content, gets their attention and finally converts their attention into a purchase from you.

An integrated view of e-mail marketing

Although e-mail marketing is an expression widely used today, it may convey a limited scope – just another expression for electronic direct mail. In fact, e-mail marketing is not only about marketing and selling through e-mail, it is about delivering *customer value* through e-mail services. Perhaps the term e-mail marketing should be replaced by e-mail services. However, we will retain e-mail marketing, emphasising the view that it relates to the broader context of delivering customer value.

E-mail marketing, therefore, is not an isolated marketing activity but an integral part of an overall e-CRM strategy. To make a difference, e-mail marketing should benefit from the integration of all customer-facing departments in your e-CRM strategy. Marketing, sales, service and support, order fulfilment and delivery should all be asked to participate and contribute to the e-mail marketing strategy. They should agree on a common strategy, adopt a common profiling mechanism, apply the same company branding to e-mail and use the same subscribe and unsubscribe routines. The customer should not receive the impression that they are dealing with different companies when they receive e-mail from different departments of your enterprise – only the content should be different. This is an important aspect of strengthening your brand through the total customer experience.

Figure 4.1 provides an overview of how integration would work. Customers use an online profiling feature that covers all aspects of e-mail marketing offered by your enterprise. When a department decides to offer e-mail marketing, it should integrate its profile options into the company-wide profile database. In the back end, departments create their own content and define the target list of recipients.

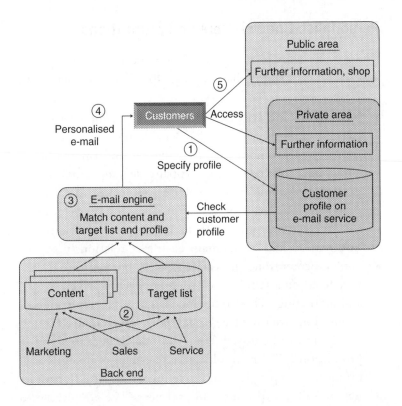

Figure 4.1: Personalised e-mail from multiple customer-facing departments features relevant content matched to target lists and profiles

The e-mail engine matches content and target lists with customer profiles and sends personalised messages that feature *all and only* the content that the individual customers have specified in their profile. If the e-mail includes an embedded link that guides the customer to the private area, the customer will be asked for their personal private area password in order to have access.

KEY CONCEPT

E-mail marketing should be an integral part of the enterprise's e-CRM strategy. All customer-facing departments should adopt a common strategy and branding for e-mail marketing.

Personalised newsletters and promotions

The scheme shown in Figure 4.1 is relevant to newsletters and e-mail campaigns that have the following characteristics:

- Newsletters are typically sent out on a regular basis (weekly, monthly, quarterly). Newsletters are educational rather than promotional in content, to inform customers about new products, new company developments, to provide tips about how to solve a problem or to show best practices. The main objective of electronic newsletters is to serve the customer with interesting and relevant information and to maintain customer relationships.
- E-mail promotions and campaigns are not typically scheduled on a regular basis, but are events driven by sales and marketing. Their frequency is not predictable unless promotions are run on a regular basis, which in itself is not a good strategy because it conditions customers to wait for promotions. The main objective of e-mail campaigns and promotions typically is to move inventory, to offer trade-ups, to sell new products and services ('We are pleased to announce a two-hour response time to your service requests at the very attractive rates shown below. You can subscribe to this great new service by simply clicking <u>here</u>').

A number of interesting personalisation scenarios can be implemented by combining e-mail marketing with a personalised web site, database synchronisation and back-end integration, as discussed before. For example:

- Dear Mrs Smith. Two years ago you purchased our product ABC. Today we are proud to present our new advanced product ABD. Please follow the link <u>Show-Me-ABD</u> to check out further details. As a special thanks for being a valued customer, your existing service contract for product ABC will be extended to cover product ABD for one year at no additional cost for the first year if you place an order for ABD by <date>.

- Dear Mr Miller. Thanks for having attended our seminar 'Introduction to Northern Italian Cuisine'. We are pleased to announce our brand new seminar, <u>Risotto Recipes from Piedmont</u>. Just follow the link above and you will be guided to your personalised web site where you can make your reservation for 15 per cent off the advertised fee.

GETTING STARTED: Personalised newsletters

Customer-driven content

One important element for the development of successful newsletters is the involvement of readers in the definition of some aspects of the content. Involving your customers in the selection of topics and even in providing content will ensure their continued interest in receiving your newsletter.

One approach is simply to invite your customers to contribute testimonials, stories or tips regarding their use of your product. You then select the best one for inclusion in your next newsletter. Besides the editorial work, this method is relatively easy to set up and often only requires a thank-you note to the contributor or a simple, inexpensive incentive.

Another approach is to let readers vote for the next story to include in your newsletter. This requires some more work on your side: within your electronic newsletter you offer an embedded link to a page in your web site where you list the titles and a one-sentence description of the candidate stories. A simple application lets readers vote and tallies the results. The winning story is published in your next newsletter. In this way you gain four benefits at the same time: (a) you learn about customer preferences directly from them; (b) you focus your resources on a subject that you know is of interest to your customers; (c) you raise your readers' expectations for your next newsletter; (d) you build better relationships with your readers by letting them interact with you through the newsletter and influence the content.

To prevent some readers casting their vote several times, you could publish the voting application in the private area where you limit voting to your known customers. There, after a customer has voted, you remove the voting application from the specific customer and display the current status of the results, with a thank-you note for having voted.

Benefits for your customers:

- They receive timely, interesting and relevant information.
- Profile options enable customers to pre-select the type of information they want to receive from the enterprise.
- In the case of customer-driven content, customers become involved and can influence the choice of content.

Benefits for your enterprise:

- Shorter time-to-customer through the speed of e-mail.
- Precision marketing by addressing only people interested in specific topics.
- Applicable to all customer-facing departments in your enterprise.
- Opportunities for up-selling and cross-selling.
- If you opt for customer-driven content, you learn what is of interest to your customers and can focus your resources on more customer-oriented content.

Notification-type e-mail

There is another type of e-mail: notification (sometimes also called 'alert'). This is event-driven e-mail, meaning that, as soon as a specific event occurs, an e-mail goes out to customers who requested to be informed about the event.

An example in the logistics area is: 'Your order status has changed. The expected delivery date is now . . .'. To enable such notification, in this example the back-end order management system would continually check if order status data change, and if they do the corresponding customers would be notified. Compared to the pull mechanism of the order status feature offered on the Web, where the customer must log in and run the feature, e-mail notification is a push mechanism that proactively informs the customer about changes.

The customer benefits in two ways: (a) they receive timely information; and (b) they need not log in the order status feature on the Web on a regular basis to see if anything has changed.

Order change notification does not replace the order status feature on the Web – it complements it. On the Web, the customer can continue to have access to an overview of a specific order or of all orders placed with the enterprise.

E-mail notification, in this example, is enabled by the integration of your back end and your web site: the back end detects an event, an e-mail notifies the customer about the event and offers a direct link to the private area, where the customer can find additional information or perform a task (see Figure 4.2).

 **GETTING STARTED:** E-mail notification

Here is an example of a more extensive use of e-mail notification in a business-to-business environment. Let us

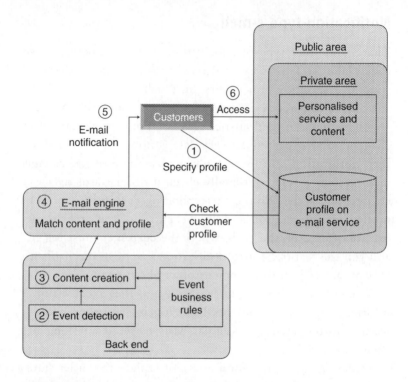

Figure 4.2: E-mail notifications inform customers about events important to them

assume that a customer has signed several different service contracts for different products in different departments in her company. The customer (Mrs Miller) has not opted for automatic contract renewal. Based on an e-mail notification service, you can offer the customer a reliable and convenient solution to extend the service contracts just in time:

1 Mrs Miller handles all the service contracts she has signed with your service department. Her private area profile specifies e-mail notification before a service contract expires.

2 Your back-end service contract application detects the event 'Service contract no. XYZ for Mrs Miller expires next month'.

3 The back-end system looks up the business rule set by the service contract manager and creates a pre-defined text to be sent to Mrs Miller.

4 The e-mail engine personalises the e-mail.

5 The e-mail engine sends out the message:

'Dear Mrs Miller. Your service contract no. XYZ expires next month. To renew it, please use the Extend my service contract feature at your personalised web site.'

6 Mrs Miller clicks on the embedded link to be guided to the appropriate application in the private area where she can extend the service contract.

Other examples of e-mail notification:

■ Your order status has changed. The new delivery date is . . . If you wish to view details or change your order, please use our Order service feature.

■ The three-year free service for your car expires three months from today. We will be pleased to check the car for you before that date to make sure everything is in order. Please visit your personalised web site and use the Schedule service routine you are already familiar with.

Benefits for your customers:

● They receive timely and precise information when the information is critical to their decision-making process.

CONTINUED . . .

Benefits for your enterprise:

- This is a feature highly valued by customers. Professional implementation will lead to increased customer satisfaction and sustain their loyalty.
- E-mail notification in conjunction with back-end integration creates new opportunities for enhancing customer relationships and for additional business.

Profiling options

All of the above will work only if customers can specify in their profile their preferences regarding content, the type of e-mail they like to receive and how often. Again as an example, Mrs Miller's profile related to the e-mail notification preferences could look as in Figure 4.3.

Perhaps you sell microwave ovens and think this does not apply to your business. What if your customers found the following note when opening a newly purchased microwave oven?

- Thank you so much for having purchased our high-quality microwave oven! To help you enjoy it for years, we have opened a web site where you can register for a monthly newsletter full of tips and recipes. Please go to http://www.greatmicrowaves.com/newsletter.
- The advanced version would be: Thank you so much for having purchased our high-quality microwave! To ensure you enjoy it for years, we are pleased to inform you about a special section of our web site full of tips available only to our valued customers. Please go to http://www.greatmicrowaves.com/privatearea, and enter the following code to get access to the restricted area. Once registered,

We offer to send you a personalised newsletter by e-mail. Please select the content you would like to receive by checking any of the following boxes:
- ☑ News about our company (press releases)
- ☑ New product announcements
- ☑ Tips and tricks about product usage
- ☐ Technical information notes
- ☑ Success stories and best practices

Do you want to be notified by e-mail if any of the following events occur? Please check all of the events you want to be notified for:
- ☑ Service contract expires
- ☐ Warranty expires
- ☑ Order status changes

When would you prefer to receive the e-mail notifications?
- ○ Immediately after the event occurred, one e-mail per event.
- ⦿ One e-mail at the end of the day covering all events occurring during the day.

If you would like to receive promotional information, please check:
- ☑ Yes, I would like to receive promotional information by e-mail.

Figure 4.3: Profile options enable customers to specify what e-mails they want to receive

you are entitled to receive a newsletter with brand new recipes every month.

On your web site you would then have the opportunity to advertise microwave accessories, other appliances or cookbooks (cross-sell).

If you serve a large business customer, you could develop another content category that features news about the ongoing relationship between your enterprise and the large account, announces customised products or talks about common events (for profile option see Figure 4.4).

The profiling concept shown above only makes sense if you have enough content for each of the listed content categories and for every e-mail edition. If you are not sure that you can provide content on a regular basis for a particular category, it would be dangerous to let the customer profile for that category. This is because, by letting customers

☑ News <our enterprise> – <your enterprise>

Figure 4.4: If you serve large accounts you can publish news about your corporation, events or customised products. With e-mail marketing you improve customer relationships

profile for a specific category, you raise the expectation that they will regularly receive that type of content.

Do not misuse customers' permission to e-mail content to them according to their category profile. Even if you have such great news in another category that you want to tell the whole world, it is extremely important to respect the customers' decision if they have not profiled for that category. They have given you permission to e-mail them specific content and that is all. Sending them content from different categories could be considered spam or junk e-mail.

Benefits for your customers:

- They receive exactly the information via e-mail that they are interested in. They can customise their profile so that the e-mail content meets their individual information needs.

Benefits for your enterprise:

- Competitive advantage and increased customer satis-faction by offering information services that the competition will find it difficult to match.

Multi-channel notification

Notification is not limited to e-mail. You could offer multiple channels to inform customers through any channel they prefer, as illustrated in Figure 4.5.

Please check preferred channels for notification:

☑ Your default e-mail address,

or specify [   ]

☐ Short Message via SMS using your default mobile phone number,

or specify [   ]

Fax to your ☐ home fax ☐ business fax,

or specify [   ]

Figure 4.5: Getting the right information at the right time is crucial. If your customers can specify how they want to receive it, you could give them a competitive advantage

Give your customers full control over what channel they can receive notification through. Let customers switch from one channel to another that serves them better whenever they change environment, whether they are in the office, on vacation or on a business trip. For example:

- I am at an offsite meeting for the next three days and will not have access to e-mail. Notifications should be sent as an SMS to my business mobile phone.
- I am on holiday in a remote island resort. My computer vendor should inform me by fax of the delivery date of my new server.

By offering such a feature you ensure that your customers do not miss the information that is important to them. The default values mentioned above refer to the standard customer profile data that customers have specified in a different section of the profiling feature. A full implementation would need to consider the different form factors and characteristics of the receiving appliances.

For example, by offering the SMS option you must keep the important part of the information to within 160 characters.

Benefits for your customers:

- High communication flexibility: customers receive notifications in time wherever they are.

Benefits for your enterprise:

- Increased customer satisfaction by meeting their information needs and their mobility requirements with timely notifications.
- Delivering on-time information to customers gives you a strong competitive advantage.

Opt-in, double opt-in and unsubscribe

Opt-in

E-mail (be it marketing, sales or service related) should be sent only to those who have requested it. This approach is called 'opt-in'. In other words, you should never send a promotional e-mail or newsletter to somebody who has not given permission for you to do so, otherwise the recipient may find the message intrusive and reject it as well as the sender.

There is possibly one exception when you would send an e-mail to someone who has not asked for it, and that is to announce your *new* e-mail marketing service to your existing customers. The justification is that these are people who already have a business relationship with you and have the right to be informed about a new benefit you offer. In this case the message must be polite, benefit oriented and short – it should not have an aggressive tone or be too long to download and read. However, even in this once-only case of non-opted-in e-mail, not all of your customers will like it, so be warned.

The process for subscribing to an e-mail marketing service should be clear to the customer. The same principles and steps as discussed in Chapter 3 (page 59 and following) apply to e-mail opt-in, so we will not repeat them. The result of the subscription process is that the customer has registered to receive your e-mail marketing service and has submitted a profile for specific fields of interests when asked to do so.

A side topic to consider here is how to ensure that customers enter the correct e-mail address. E-mail addresses can be misspelled, particularly if they are long, and customers can and will enter a wrong address by mistake. This will result in non-delivery notification from the mail server, which would be a pity for a customer who has expressed interest in your e-mail marketing service. A typo can lose you a prospect. How can you avoid this? An effective solution is to ask for the e-mail address twice. In the same way that you ask for the password twice when you first register the customer, so you ask for the e-mail address twice, the application compares the two fields and if they differ the customer corrects the address. This, of course, is an extra step for the customer, but making sure that the e-mail address is correct is worth the effort. A short explanation next to the fields will help the customer understand why.

Double opt-in

While the opt-in process is usually a straightforward process, there is the possibility of misuse: if you offer the registration feature to the public, someone could register another person by entering that person's data, such as name and e-mail address, without authorisation. If you accept the data as it is and proceed to send e-mail, you are effectively spamming that person. A 'double opt-in' avoids this misuse but requires an additional step. After registration, you send a personalised welcome message to the registered person and at the same time ask for a specific action to confirm that the recipient wants to be registered for the e-mail marketing service. The action could be to reply to the welcome message or follow an embedded link. If the recipient does not confirm, you delete their e-mail address from your database and you will not spam them.

If on the one hand the double opt-in approach helps avoid misuse, on the other it could result in fewer subscribers:

- If the confirmation procedure is not explained very well people could be confused; if they don't know what to do, they won't follow the procedure.
- If the confirmation procedure is not easy to follow, people could abort the confirmation.
- If the recipients do not read the welcome message or merely skip the confirmation procedure description, they will fail to confirm; they will believe they are registered but in fact are not.
- It may be perceived by your customers as an additional burden.

Of course, double opt-in is not necessary if you offer the e-mail service to known customers who are already registered for your private area services.

Unsubscribe

It is not only important to make it easy and convenient to subscribe, it is equally important to make it easy and convenient to unsubscribe:

- If the reader is not satisfied with the e-mail service and does not know how to unsubscribe, any additional e-mail will cause irritation, if not anger.
- If the unsubscribe process is complicated, the readers might abort and with the next unwanted e-mail you would effectively spam them.
- If your customers receive unsolicited e-mail they could add you to their e-mail filter, so that any of your messages thereafter would be deleted before even reaching the customer's in-tray.
- On the positive side, a customer who unsubscribes might still continue to do business with you and an easy unsubscribe process is a positive experience.

There are multiple options on how to make it easy to unsubscribe. Every e-mail from the e-mail marketing service should close with an explanation of how to do it and offer one of these options:

- An embedded link that directly performs the unsubscription.
- An embedded link leading to the appropriate profiling section in the private area. Here the customer can change the profile.
- A telephone number that leads to contact centre agents who can execute the process.
- A fax number or e-mail address to which the customer can send notification to unsubscribe.

Benefits for your customers:

- Customers have the power to decide when to receive and when to discontinue the service.

CONTINUED . . .

Benefits for your enterprise:

- Your service reaches only those who have asked for it and you avoid spamming which could otherwise cause you legal problems.
- An easy opt-in feature increases the probability of more people subscribing to your services.
- An easy opt-out or unsubscribe process need not lose you an existing customer.

Single messages

In addition to delivering regular e-mail marketing services, organisations can provide value by fulfilling single-shot requests for information. These requests can be stimulated for the purpose of developing new prospects.

For example, on your public web site you could offer an article, a research paper or other valuable information via e-mail to visitors, and all they have to do to receive the information is to give their e-mail address.

At this stage it is wise to make it clear that visitors' e-mail addresses will be used only to send the requested information. Visitors who are afraid you would sell their e-mail address to other companies and who do not wish to receive unsolicited promotional information will not supply their addresses, so potential new prospects will be lost. If in addition to the e-mail address you ask for the customer's name and physical location details, you should leave those fields optional and should give visitors very good reasons for that information being necessary.

From the enterprise's standpoint the motivation is clear: 'We have invested in the white paper, it contains valuable data and knowledge; so if somebody wants to receive it the deal is: research paper against reader information'. The visitor, especially someone who is not familiar with your enterprise, has a different motivation. All they want is to get the offered information, but they also understand that behind the offer there might be a marketing ploy to sell something later. An enterprise that spends money on advertising does not ask readers to release personal data for the privilege of reading the ads. So from the visitor's viewpoint there is no clear reason for the enterprise to be asking for more data in the scenario described above. If you entered a restaurant and asked to see the full menu but the waiter at the entrance would let you see it only if you supplied your name and address, would you comply or walk out? An enterprise that sets up a deal-oriented feature on its site misses the visitor's viewpoint, which is in fact the visitor's deal: 'I'll continue to talk to you only if I don't have to release any additional data.'

For this very reason, we think it is almost self-explanatory, using the example above, that you should not ask the visitor to subscribe to a newsletter in order to receive the research paper. Even if you claim that your newsletter is the best in your industry, there will be people who will not want to receive it – at least not now, when they do not know your company yet. The alternative is to provide, next to the offer of the research paper, a check box or an optional field where visitors can subscribe to the newsletter. If they do so and conclude that the newsletter offers interesting information and do not unsubscribe soon after, then you may have the opportunity to ask for more information.

From the e-CRM viewpoint, once the customer has entered their e-mail address, the enterprise should fulfil the request immediately – not the next day or the next week. The e-mail should thank the visitor for the interest expressed, point to the attached file containing the requested infor- mation and offer further ways to receive additional information (if applicable) by subscribing to a newsletter or by registering on the web site.

Benefits for visitors:

- They can receive offered information of value to them without being asked to release further data about themselves.

Benefits for your enterprise:

- Win new prospects.
- Gain trust by respecting visitors' privacy.

Measurement and tracking

The results of an e-mail campaign can be analysed more effectively than those of a traditional paper mail campaign. As soon as the e-mail gets into the recipient's inbox, depending on what e-mail application you use, you could find answers to questions such as:

- How many people have opened your message? This could be an indicator of how interesting your overall e-mail is.
- How many people have clicked on the embedded links (response rate)? This could be an indicator of how interesting a specific topic is.
- How many people clicked through to the shopping application? This information could be related to the number of purchases (conversion rate).

The results in terms of numbers (how many) tell you if the topic you promoted was of interest to your target group.

However, they don't say anything about the quality of your topics and if you met your customer expectations. In Chapter 6 we will show how to collect qualitative data.

If your system enables you to track the behaviour of individual recipients (who has opened the message or clicked on an embedded link), you can use this information to update your customer databases or the customer's web profile to improve the personalisation they will experience in the future.

A professional e-mail marketing approach requires the feedback of rigorous measurement. The measures that are appropriate for your environment should be defined before selecting the optimal e-mail engine application. Among the multiple features an e-mail engine offers there should be an extensive tracking capability, because from it you will learn how to improve your e-mail services.

Here are some examples of tracking capabilities offered by existing e-mail marketing applications:

- Opened messages: how many recipients have opened your message, who and when.
- Clickthroughs: how many recipients have clicked on an embedded link, who, when and which link.
- Undeliverable messages ('bounces') due to, for example, invalid e-mail address or hardware failure.
- Store the tracking results in files or sheets for further processing.

Benefits to your customers:

- Tracking and measurement ultimately lead to a better customer experience with e-mail marketing services.

CONTINUED . . .

Benefits to your enterprise:

- Tracking and measurement help you understand how many of your readers you reach, how interesting your content is etc. This enables you to improve your e-mail service over time and serve customers better.

Inbound e-mail management

Until now we have discussed how best to send messages to customers. Now let's turn the subject around and focus on how best to deal with messages coming from customers. This is such a great opportunity to satisfy customers' needs and to win new customers (*they contact* the enterprise, *they ask* for sales information, they have a problem *you can solve*) that it should motivate companies to do the best possible job at answering inbound e-mail. Unfortunately, many companies only see the workload caused by inbound e-mail, fail to understand the opportunities hidden in those messages and do not make the effort to respond promptly and accurately. Prompt, courteous and competent answers can have a higher impact on customer loyalty and can win new customers more effectively than advertising or mailing campaigns. However, the lack of appropriate performance measures often prevents marketing and service people from investing in this area.

Customers expect a prompt reply to their e-mail messages, whether they are seeking information, submitting a problem or asking for a return phone call from the enterprise's sales staff. Their expectation of speed of response to e-mail is close to that of a phone call, not to that of physical mail. There is no point in sitting on e-mail for days.

Waiting too long before responding to e-mail, or not responding at all, will be interpreted as unfriendly, uncaring or disrespectful behaviour. If your enterprise is among those that do not perform well in this area, don't just blame your people. If your enterprise is not yet prepared to receive and promptly respond to customers' e-mails, you must first define responsibilities and set up the processes and tools to deal professionally with the growing load of inbound messages.

The messages we are referring to are not those going to specific people in the enterprise (e.g. sales reps or service engineers whose e-mail addresses is on their business cards). These are messages that go to generic addresses such as info@. . ., webmaster@. . . or customerservice@. . . . Customers usually find these addresses on the enterprise's web site or in brochures and ads.

For every generic e-mail address offered (an e-mail address that is not associated with one individual person in the enterprise), there should be a process defining whose responsibility it is to check incoming messages and to whom the message should be escalated if it cannot be immediately and completely answered. It is very important to have such a process for all generic addresses offered by the enterprise. One cannot be sure that the customer knows where to send the message: to info@. . . or to webmaster@. . . or customerservice@. . . . If the customer sends e-mail to the 'wrong' address, it is not the customer's fault.

It is the responsibility of the department or individual at the receiving end to take care of re-routing and send an acknowledgement to the customer that the e-mail was received and the request is being dealt with. Additional information such as who is handling the enquiry and when to expect an answer will help reassure the customer. This may seem very basic correspondence etiquette, yet it is often ignored because the immediacy of the medium may make it

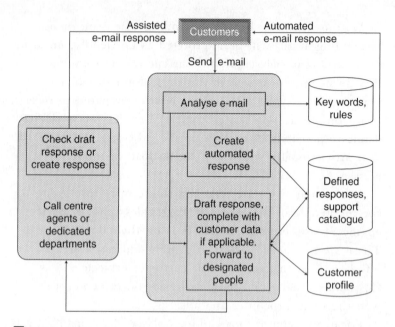

Figure 4.6: E-mail response tools enable automated and assisted responses

appear redundant when in fact it is just as necessary in the case of physical mail.

In the case of large amounts of incoming messages an enterprise could deploy a tool that supports automated or rule-assisted answers. Such a tool or application checks the incoming messages and, if it detects certain pre-defined key words, runs a search in the support database (which could be the same database available to customers on the web site), selects the top one or ten answers and sends an e-mail back to the customer. If no automatic answer is possible because, for example, key words like 'service request' or 'problem' are found in the customer's message, the tool routes the message to the customer service department without delay. In addition, an auto-response routine informs the customer that the message was received and is being handled promptly. Figure 4.6 gives a simplified overview of how such tools work.

Automatic answering could also be configured as an extra service to offer customers. When a customer sends an e-mail with a specific key word ('press release', 'promotion' etc.) in the subject field to a specific address such as mailservice@. . ., the application searches the web database, extracts the most recent content related to the key word, creates an e-mail and sends it back to the customer.

In a more personalised and elaborate version of this service, the application recognises a 'most valued customer' from the e-mail address, places the request on top of the process stack and copies the incoming message with the reply to the appropriate customer service agent for follow-up.

The benefit for customers is that they do not have to log on to your web site (enter user ID, password, then select the appropriate feature). All they have to do is send a short e-mail and within seconds they get a response displaying the requested information. This type of automatic e-mail service is viable if the information provided is not confidential to customers. Confidential information should not travel via e-mail on the Internet – experienced hackers could get hold of the information before it arrives in the recipient's e-mail inbox.

Benefits for your customers:

- They receive prompt answers to their enquiries in a convenient way.

Benefits for your enterprise:

- You improve customer satisfaction by promptly responding to their messages.
- You can reduce inbound workload by automating the process.
- Prompt, competent answers can motivate customers to purchase from you and not from the competition.

Boost direct marketing with e-mail marketing

Not all enterprises want or can communicate only through e-mail. Not all customers want to receive e-mail only. Physical mail will continue to have a role to play in direct marketing. The likely scenario for the future is that e-mail marketing is run together with physical mail direct marketing, but gradually takes a larger share of CRM communications as it demonstrates greater efficiencies and better sales results.

> **KEY CONCEPT**
>
> The sample calculation shows that e-mail marketing needs an up-front investment, but using it means that sales and marketing efficiency can increase dramatically.

In order to show the benefits of integration we created a CRM business model with a sample calculation for a fictitious enterprise, Genius & Co. As all enterprises operate in different environments, have different marketing strategies and sell different products to different customers, the simulation can only be viewed as an example. But we think it could be used as a model for your own calculation, where the final figures will depend on your own situation and requirements.

Case Study: Genius & Co.

A sample calculation

The computations in Table 4.1 are based on the following assumptions:

- One of Genius & Co's primary objectives is to increase sales. Direct marketing has been part of the sales strategy for years. Can e-mail marketing increase sales and at the same time improve the overall efficiency of CRM communications? The calculation should demonstrate it.

Table 4.1: Integrated e-mail marketing generates higher marketing efficiency

Genius & Co	Traditional direct mail marketing				E-mail marketing		
	Year 0	Year 1	Year 2	Year 3	Year 1	Year 2	Year 3
Customer address database							
New prospects	3 000	3 000	2 000	1 000	1 000	2 000	4 000
Customers switching to e-mail service					3 000	5 000	7 000
Customer address database	100 000	100 000	97 000	91 000	4 000	11 000	22 000
Purchase rate (success rate)							
Response rate per campaign	1.5%	1.5%	1.5%	1.5%	15%	20%	22%
Conversion rate	90%	90%	90%	90%	10%	12%	14%
Purchase rate	1.4%	1.4%	1.4%	1.4%	1.5%	2.4%	3.1%
Products sold per campaign							
Target as % of customer base	40%	40%	40%	40%	25%	20%	15%
Number targeted	40 000	40 000	38 800	36 400	1 000	2 200	3 300
Up-sell and cross-sell	0%	0%	0%	0%	10%	10%	20%
Products sold per campaign	540	540	524	491	17	58	122
Costs per campaign							
Unit mail cost	$1.00	$1.00	$1.00	$1.00	$0.20	$0.15	$0.10
Mailing cost	$40 000	$40 000	$38 800	$36 400	$200	$330	$330
Mail piece creation	$3 000	$3 000	$3 000	$3 000	$2 000	$1 500	$1 500
Total cost per campaign	$43 000	$43 000	$41 800	$39 400	$2 200	$1 830	$1 830
Campaigns per year							
Number of campaigns	10	10	10	10	20	30	40
Mail pieces sent	400 000	400 000	388 000	364 000	20 000	66 000	132 000
All campaign costs per year	$430 000	$430 000	$418 000	$394 000	$44 000	$54 900	$73 200

continued overleaf

Table 4.1: (continued)

Genius & Co	Traditional direct mail marketing			E-mail marketing		
Other costs per year						
Gain new addresses, win prospects	$10 000		$8 000	$15 000	$10 000	$10 000
Set up service				$10 000		
Web site features development				$15 000		$5 000
Design layout and template	$2 000		$2 000	$5 000	$2 000	$2 000
Mail merge, bounces, dedups				$10 000		$5 000
Campaign management headcount	$80 000		$80 000	$80 000		$80 000
CRM e-mail content headcount				$30 000		$40 000
Other costs per year	$92 000		$90 000	$165 000	$150 000	$142 000
Totals per year						
Costs	$522 000	$508 000	$484 000	$209 000	$204 900	$215 200
Products sold	5 400	5 238	4 914	330	1 742	4 879
Customer penetration	4	4	4	5	6	6

Paper mail plus e-mail

Integrated results	Year 0	Year 1	Year 2	Year 3
Products sold	5 400	5 730	6 980	9 793
Marketing costs	$522 000	$731 000	$712 900	$699 200
Marketing costs per product sold	97	128	102	71
Customer address database	100 000	104 000	108 000	113 000
Average purchase rate	5.40%	5.51%	6.46%	8.67%

CONTINUED . . . Case Study: Genius & Co.

- Genius & Co will not replace its traditional paper mail campaigns with e-mail marketing. E-mail marketing will be added to its current campaign activities; traditional direct marketing will gradually be reduced as e-mail marketing proves to be efficient.
- One of the communication objectives is that every customer will receive at least four promotional mailings per year. The mailings shall also reinforce brand awareness.
- The customer address database for the e-mail service will include only people who have given their permission to receive promotional e-mail.
- Some of the customers currently receiving direct mail from Genius & Co will switch from paper mail to e-mail. A customer who opts for e-mail will no longer receive paper mail. It is expected that the majority of the new prospects won by Genius & Co will subscribe to the e-mail marketing service. The e-mail subscribers have the choice between ASCII (plain text) and HTML e-mail (with hypertext links to relevant parts of the web site and possibly including pictures etc.).
- An enterprise web site exists and offers a private area with basic profiling features. Genius & Co's IT people have adequate knowledge of e-mail technology.
- The sample calculation should be applicable to both in-house and outsourced services.

Year 0 Zero base: Genius & Co runs traditional paper mail marketing without any e-mail marketing activities.
New prospects Number of prospects that Genius & Co wins due to marketing communication activities, word of mouth etc.

CONTINUED . . . Case Study: Genius & Co.

Customers switching to e-mail service   Genius & Co customers who opt for e-mail. They do not receive paper mail any more.

Customer address database   Number of addresses in the customer database(s) with customer permission to mail to them.

Response rate per campaign   Paper: percentage of customers who contact Genius & Co (phone, fax, reply card) to receive more product information or to order. E-mail: percentage of customers who click on the e-mail embedded link (clickthrough) leading to the Genius & Co web site for more product information.

Conversion rate   Paper: percentage of customers who responded and purchased. E-mail: percentage of customers who clicked through and purchased.

Purchase rate   Percentage of mail recipients who purchase (response rate × conversion rate).

Targets as % of customer base   Percentage of addresses that will receive the mail.

Up-sell and cross-sell   Percentage of customers who purchase two products instead of one due to the mailing.

Unit mail cost   Paper: print, mailing and overhead costs. E-mail: internal or external service costs.

Mailing cost   Number of targets × unit mail cost.

Mail piece creation   Content creation and adaptation to the flyer template/e-mail template. Proofreading.

Mail pieces sent   Total number of mail pieces sent out.

Gain new addresses, win prospects   Activities to gain new prospects and add their addresses to the customer database, if permitted.

CONTINUED . . . Case Study: Genius & Co.

Setup service   Once-only costs to pay an external or internal service provider to set up e-mail marketing and interface to IT processes.

Web site features development   Application development effort to develop subscribe/unsubscribe features, profile options and internal and/or external processes.

Design layout and template   Agency or internal effort to design layout of campaign flyer/HTML message and create the appropriate template.

Mail merge, bounces, deduplication   Costs to cover all items needed to technically merge addresses and text, personalise messages, manage bounces after mailing is sent and clean addresses if necessary.

Campaign management headcount   Headcount costs to manage and run all activities, including planning, introducing, running and analysing campaigns.

CRM e-mail content headcount   Headcount costs to develop the additional content and text needed to create personalised messages.

Customer penetration   Number of mail pieces that one customer receives on average per year.

Average purchase rate   Percentage of customers who purchase one product over the year.

Interpreting the results:

- Genius & Co needs to make an investment decision for both headcount and internal or external service providers.
- The investment in year 1 clearly does not pay off in year 1. Sales only increase slightly and costs per product sold are 25 per cent higher than with paper mail only.

CONTINUED . . . Case Study: Genius & Co.

- Costs per product sold in year 2 are still higher than with paper mail, but sales increase significantly.
- E-mail marketing pays off in year 3: sales increase again, costs per product sold are significantly lower than with paper mail, the customer address base has wider coverage and average customer penetration increases from four to six times a year.

Campaign management

CHAPTER 5

Overview

This chapter highlights professional campaign management principles:

- Selecting the best strategy to focus on the right customers.
- Developing the right campaign plan and executing it.
- Installing a powerful tracking capability to measure success and to learn how to improve.

E-mail or web campaigns require the same level of professional planning and execution as traditional media campaigns. The ease, immediacy and comparably lower cost with which electronic campaigns can be implemented should not detract from applying the same standards as a professional campaign, if not even higher quality. If customers receive do-it-yourself, low-quality e-mail, they may delete all future e-mail messages from the same source without reading them.

The flexibility of the electronic tools available allows multiple ways of preparing and running campaigns. In this chapter we will discuss three electronic campaign approaches:

the single-level campaign or the pre-tested on-shot campaign via e-mail and/or Web; the multi-level campaign featuring different follow-up alternatives depending on the customer's response to the previous campaign step; and, last but not least, how to improve the response rate.

The combination of e-mail marketing and a personalised web site offers the greatest flexibility for running campaigns.

Single-level campaigns

Campaign preparation

As an example of a single-level campaign, you are preparing a campaign code named 'Gold Promotion' where the targets are your most valuable customers (code named 'Gold customers') who will receive an e-mail announcing a new product offered with a special Gold customer incentive. The e-mail includes an embedded link that guides customers to the private area where they can find further information and an ordering feature.

You start by defining the target group using the information in your back-end customer databases or in your web customer database. Data analysis and data mining can be applied to extract the target group, as we will also discuss in Chapter 6. In this example the selection criteria could be: all customers flagged as Gold customers AND have purchased product ABC in the past three years AND have given permission to receive offers or promotions AND have registered in the private area. This results in a list of recipients.

Next you define the content of the offer (title, copy, graphics, type and value of time-limited incentive) and the personalisation level, such as personalised salutation and a transaction-related message ('you purchased product ABC three years ago'). These definitions are translated into business rules that dynamically build the content appearing in the private area when selected customers click on the e-mail embedded link.

The campaign should be subjected to a quality assurance process that proofreads all content visible to customers, checks customer selection criteria and business rules, tests the campaign to see if it works as predicted and checks for viruses.

Test

In this example, the campaign is tested by sending it to test addresses that simulate customers set up in the private area featuring the relevant customer profiles. The test procedure should cover the complete process: send the e-mail, see how customers would receive it, follow the embedded link to the private area, check if and how the promotional content pops up and if the special incentive is applied. If the body of the message is in HTML, the procedure should verify that the campaign works with different e-mail clients, that messages and graphics are displayed correctly, and test how long it takes for it to be downloaded through low-bandwidth connections. In addition, the procedure should verify that the campaign's web content is not visible to customers who are not included in the e-mail selection list.

Execute and track

If the campaign passes the tests, you schedule it, run it, track the activity (how many customers followed the embedded link, how many purchased the offer) and analyse the results, as discussed in Chapter 5 (page 124).

Manage bounces

When you send an e-mail that cannot be delivered, your system receives a message listing the recipient and the reason that the e-mail did not reach the customer's inbox. This type of message is called a 'bounce'. This is normally not a problem with business customers, unless the recipient has left the company. It could be a problem with consumers if they switch their e-mail service provider so that your e-mail is not delivered. Your customer information management process should decide whether to recover a valid e-mail address through other means (because in our example we are dealing with Gold customers) or merely delete it from your data sources.

Technical prerequisites

The components of the system on which you run e-mail or web campaigns will need to be operational before you run your first campaign. The e-mail and web applications should be designed or selected to support the required features of the chosen process, for example the one outlined above. If you send HTML e-mail, you must take care over the design and layout of the HTML body. The customer profile and/or back-end customer databases should support the targeted customer selections and, last but not least, follow-up processes need to be set up.

Time-to-customer

While traditional paper mail campaigns take weeks to execute, e-mail/Web-based campaigns take days. Unless you are keen to incorporate sophisticated graphics in HTML e-mail or on the Web, it may take two to three days maximum to prepare and run a campaign.

Benefits for your customers:

- Customers who have given permission to be sent promotional information receive tailored offers and timely information about new products and services.
- The private area gives customers an efficient and secure way to examine offers and make purchase decisions.

Benefits to your enterprise:

- Short time-to-customer when running campaigns. This gives you a strong competitive advantage when announcing new products or promotions.
- Increased sales based on precise target marketing.
- Immediate tracking and measurements are possible for quickly improving your campaigns.
- The flexibility and power of Web-based/e-mail-based techniques make it possible to run more and better-focused campaigns than with traditional media.

Multi-level, multi-channel campaigns

A multi-level campaign consists of different consecutive steps based on the individual customer's responses or click-throughs following the initial message.

Let's say that we run the Gold Promotion described in the previous section as a multi-level campaign with up to four levels:

- *Level 1* Customers receive the e-mail campaign message described above.
- *Level 2* All customers who have received the Level 1 message but did not click on the embedded link receive a

second e-mail referring to the previous one and emphasising the benefits of the promotion.

- *Level 3* Customers who used the embedded link to view more detailed product information on the Web but did not order the product receive an e-mail including a choice of three different actions through embedded links. If customers select the first option, they receive an e-mail containing a complete product brochure in electronic format. The second option offers a hard-copy product brochure. If customers choose the third option, they receive a call from a call centre agent to discuss any questions they may have. Remember, these are Gold customers.

- *Level 4* All customers who purchase the promoted upgrade receive a thank-you message.

To enable this type of multi-level campaign, your e-mail and web applications must track customers' e-mail and web actions and must feed this information back into your campaign management tool.

This example also illustrates the integration between different channels: electronic (e-mail, Web), traditional mail (hard-copy brochure) and call centre agent. Multi-channel campaigns are more complex and more expensive to run than purely electronic ones, but you can serve customers with different communication media preferences and in the case of well-targeted, high-value customers the ROI can justify the expense.

Benefits for your customers:

- Customers receive tailored offers through their preferred channel.

- Multi-level campaigns provide options to gain additional information.

Benefits for your enterprise:

- Multi-level campaigns allow for non-intrusive, professional follow-up and improved customer satisfaction.
- A multi-channel strategy gives the advantage of a combination of different channels that complement each other to meet customer preferences.

Maximise the response rate

E-mail, like traditional paper mail, gives you one chance to send a message to and get a response from the targeted audience. If the message is good (relevant, interesting, timely), you may succeed. If the message is bad, you fail.

In theory, if the first campaign was not a hit, you could start all over again soon after thanks to the flexibility of the electronic tools. But the danger of annoying customers with multiple campaigns is high. It is best to design and run campaigns that have the best chance of succeeding at the outset. These are the campaigns with the best response rates.

One recommended way to maximise the response rate is to test campaign alternatives before executing the final campaign to the entire target group:

- Randomly select out of your overall target group, say, three smaller test customer groups (groups 1, 2 and 3).
- For each test group you create one common body of text with a variation of the offer, giving three different versions of the campaign (versions A, B and C).

- Next, send version A to group 1, version B to group 2 and version C to group 3.
- Within a few days you will be able to determine which version generated the highest response rate.
- You can then build your campaign around the most successful version.

The test scenario above focuses on e-mail campaigns, but can be transferred easily to any other electronic publishing medium that allows tracking.

If you consider testing as an essential component of your electronic campaign design, you will be adding a few days to the total time and still be way ahead of traditional media campaigns in terms of cycle time.

Benefits for your customers:

- Customers get offers that really meet their needs.

Benefits for your enterprise:

- Better response rate = more sales.

Closing the loop

CHAPTER 6

Overview

To complete the loop, in this chapter we discuss:

- How to gain feedback and learn from customers.
- How to consolidate and analyse customer data and turn it into a competitive advantage.
- How to co-operate with the distribution channels so that both your company and your channel can profit from e-CRM.

Learning from and about customers

Managing customer feedback

CRM cannot function without customer feedback. By feedback we do not just mean the occasional, *ad hoc* comment from customers, but rather the process that closes and completes the electronic relationship loop. The feedback process covers all the steps from planning and executing surveys, to collecting, analysing and interpreting data, and then passing the knowledge on to the relevant departments to improve the total customer experience.

Before going into more detail, there is one guiding principle to be aware of: *it should always be possible and easy for customers to give feedback*. If the customer is not provided with an easy way to give unsolicited feedback, if the survey is too long or too complicated, if the questions are unclear or unjustified, the customer simply will not do it and an opportunity for gaining customer knowledge will be lost.

We distinguish between three types of feedback option that an enterprise can make available to customers: generic feedback, context-sensitive feedback and single-topic feedback. All three should be made available, although the minimum is to offer the generic feedback option.

In this chapter we will not cover the structure of questionnaires: the optimum number of questions, open and closed questions, positioning and sequence of questions, role of free comment space etc. We will focus on how to make it easy for customers to give feedback and more efficient for the enterprise to obtain feedback, process and distribute it to the appropriate departments to learn from it.

The generic feedback option

This option is given to customers to enable them to offer feedback at any time on any subject. There is no obligation for the customer to give feedback; the customer is not asked to reply to a questionnaire. The feature is simply made available by the enterprise and made known to the customers, but the enterprise does not push customers to use it. In the electronic world every communication channel should offer the customer the option to comment, commend or complain and to ask questions. If the customer receives an e-mail message, the e-mail should include a feedback address. If the customer visits the enterprise web site, they should easily find the feedback feature. The approach is similar to listing a phone number in a printed brochure or on a web page – it is completely up to the customer to use it or not.

The most common feedback feature in a web site is a published e-mail address – by clicking on that address the customer's e-mail client is activated and the visitor can write and send an e-mail. This feature is easy to implement and widely used in the public domain.

In a CRM environment where customers are registered in the private area, the e-mail feature cannot offer the advantages of a more personalised tool: the pre-filled feedback form published in the private area. The e-mail feature requires the user to fill in both personal and feedback-related information in order for the process to log, track and later respond. In a true CRM web site, once a customer is logged into the private area, all the customer data is known to the web application. So, when the customer opens the feedback form, the appropriate customer data is retrieved from the customer profile database and filled in on the form. The profile data used for pre-filling can include customer name, other demographic data and preferred communication channel, such as e-mail address or phone number. Beyond writing the feedback comment, the customer is always entitled to change the pre-filled data. Both the customer and the enterprise benefit from this approach: the customer is recognised by the application and only has to write the feedback; and the enterprise receives useful and correct information and updated customer data if the customer modifies some of the fields.

One challenge with generic feedback is who to send it to in the organisation. Most often an e-mail will require some manual processing before being routed to the appropriate agent or department. A private area form, depending on the importance of the customer coded in the customer profile, could be directly routed to a designated agent or department.

The context-sensitive feedback option

This is a more advanced option that is best described in the context of the private area, when the front-end web application is integrated with the back-end systems. Let's say that a customer, who has registered in the private area, is reading a research paper, or checking their order status, or examining a special offer, and they have a query or comment related to the object they are currently viewing. The context-sensitive feedback option can be offered through a feedback button next to the object under examination.

When the customer pushes the button, the system opens up the feedback form and automatically pre-fills it with context-sensitive data such as research title, order number or campaign code, in addition to the relevant customer data. All the customer has to do is to enter the query or the comment, nothing more.

In addition to the convenience for the customer, the enterprise receives the benefit that the customer feedback can be routed directly to a pre-defined content owner, department or service agent group, without delays and errors.

Figure 6.1 illustrates the context-sensitive feedback option.

1 In the private area, customer Joe Smith looks at promotion campaign information related to a new mobile phone that the enterprise is promoting. The campaign is published in Joe Smith's private area because of his profile data. Joe has a question and clicks the feedback button next to the campaign text. In this example, the 'context' is the promotion campaign about which Joe has a question.

2 The feedback button opens a feedback form and pre-fills specific fields: customer name, e-mail address, home phone and daytime phone numbers, all of which are retrieved from the customer profile database. Joe's profile also indicates that e-mail is his preferred communication channel. All Joe has do is enter his question.

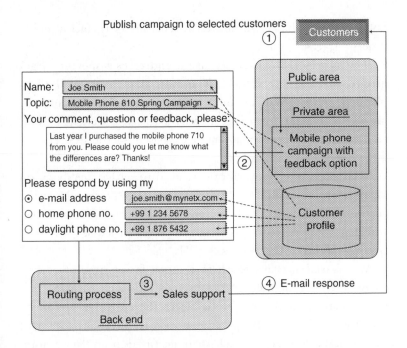

Figure 6.1: The pre-filled feedback form motivates the customer to contact you. And each contact is a chance to sell and to serve

3 After Joe has written his question, the form is automatically routed to sales support, which deals with campaign questions.

4 Sales support sends the appropriate answer via e-mail to Joe, as this is his preferred communication channel.

The focused survey option

Customers who take the initiative of asking questions or giving feedback activate the two feedback mechanisms described above. In this third option it is the enterprise that asks for feedback and pushes questions to the customers. It is in fact a focused, single-topic survey with just one or a few questions that is submitted to customers for a limited time.

The survey is focused because it addresses a specific target group with a single subject. Therefore it must be well planned, with tested, unambiguous questions, if the enterprise is to benefit from it. Customers will also benefit if their feedback influences management decisions in the desired direction.

Web survey techniques can be used to gather feedback on many subjects of interest to the enterprise: to learn about the customer experience with the enterprise's products, services and departments; to improve products or processes; or to compare alternative choices.

Web-based surveys result in a much faster time-to-customer: once defined and translated into web format, the survey can be made clearly visible to the customer the next time they visit the web site. In contrast, traditional paper mail surveys take longer to reach their destination and may not even make the customer's 'in' basket.

 ## IMPLEMENTATION CHECKLIST: Web surveys

There are a number of factors to be aware of when designing surveys for the Web:

- The first challenge is to limit the questions to the essential ones. It is too easy to add questions to web surveys: it doesn't seem to cost anything (other than for processing time) to add just a few more when compared with paper surveys. However, the flip-side of this reasoning is that users are only a click away from more interesting pursuits – the challenge is to keep them motivated not to leave the survey before completing it. Therefore 'KISS it' – Keep It Short and Simple.

◆ One advantage of paper surveys is that they will be seen when they land on the customer's desk. But if customers do not visit the web site for a while or do not enter the area where you publish the web survey, they will not see it. This is why every web survey should be promoted to customers, emphasising the importance of their contribution.

◆ Web surveys cause customers to be online for the time required to fill in the survey. This costs them time and money that they could spend elsewhere. The web survey promotion should feature a welcoming invitation and should spell out enough good arguments to motivate customers to complete the survey.

◆ Because of the speed, flexibility and lower costs offered by web survey techniques, different departments in the enterprise will become interested in launching more frequent customer surveys. In order not to overwhelm or irritate customers with multiple surveys at the same time, it is important to set up a process that approves and co-ordinates all web survey initiatives.

As in the case of generic and context-sensitive feedback, the power of single-topic web surveys comes with integration and personalisation. Define the right target group and select the customers who should have access to the survey in the private area. If you have an integrated environment (Web to back end), you could publish very focused surveys to selected customers:

■ Dear Mr Smith. A month ago you ordered our new mobile phone 810. We very much value your opinion and would like to learn how satisfied you are with the product. Would you please spend a few minutes filling in our short questionnaire.

■ Dear Mrs Miller. Your service agreement number xyz123 expired last month and was not extended. Because of your long history as a valued customer of our company, we would very much like to know your assessment of the service you received before its expiration. Would you please spend a few minutes . . .

You could also send this text in an e-mail featuring an embedded link to the private area. In our example, both Mr Smith and Mrs Miller receive a personalised invitation based on both demographic and transactional data. When customers follow the invitation, a pre-filled survey form pops up in the private area making it more convenient to fill in the survey. And because they answer in the private area, neither Mr Smith nor Mrs Miller will know that at the same time you are sending the same survey to many other customers who also purchased the mobile phone 810 or did not extend their service contract.

Opt-in surveys

Surveys represent extra work for the recipients, who need to decide if and when to take time to fill in the answers. As in the case of opt-in e-mail marketing, an enterprise could, and perhaps should, apply a policy of publishing surveys only to customers who gave permission to receive them. All it takes is a profile option in the private area that identifies customers who have indicated their willingness to participate in surveys. This approach at first reduces the number of customers who receive the survey, but the impact is not negative for the success of the survey. Those recipients who are neither willing nor interested in participating in surveys would not fill them in anyway, so the benefit for the enterprise is to avoid dissatisfying them by pushing a survey to them that they would not consider.

Another reason to adopt opt-in surveys is the limited area available on the screen. Every visible link, banner and button on a web page takes space and therefore pushes away other web page elements. If a survey link or button is not published to a visitor, the equivalent space is available for other purposes.

Product design surveys

Testing new product design concepts with experienced customers is a good practice to help ensure the success of product development. Testing new product designs or product improvements through web surveys does not replace focus groups but for certain categories of products and services it can give the advantages of flexibility and speed. Ideally, the customers to be selected, from those who have opted-in for surveys, are the loyal ones who have declared an interest in new product development in their profile. They form a community of users that are willing to invest their time to provide feedback and who have signed a non-disclosure agreement with the enterprise.

The scenario shown in Figure 6.2 could be executed within days or hours, depending on the type of product involved, and could deliver in-time feedback to product development.

1 Target customers for the survey are selected by product development based on their profile and are members of the new product development community.
2 All customers who are members of the community receive an e-mail inviting them to join the survey.
3 Customers click on an e-mail-embedded link that guides them to the private area and pops up the survey. The

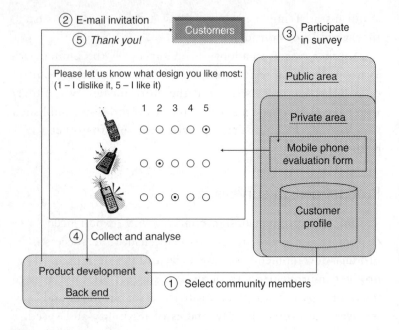

Figure 6.2: New product development supported by in-time customer feedback delivers market-focused products and ultimately higher sales

survey features mobile phone design alternatives presenting pictures and ranking options next to each.

4   Customer responses are collected at the back end and analysed. Within days or hours, product development receives valuable customer feedback on the chosen design alternatives.

5   As a follow-up (always required), product development sends a thank-you message to participating customers and, optionally, presenting the results of the survey.

Would customers be interested in participating in this kind of survey and indicate it in their profile? Some will not – but some will. Those who will are likely to be among the more loyal customers of the enterprise. They will spend their time on the survey because they feel they are being listened to and because they expect eventually to benefit from new products whose design they have influenced.

In this concept, the value of replies to the survey does not come so much from their statistical significance (which cannot be ignored), but from the experience of the customers surveyed with the product category. This also limits the applicability of this type of survey to subjects where customers have experience. New technology developments, where the offer in fact creates the demand, will not benefit from this type of survey.

GETTING STARTED: Principles for managing feedback

Ask for feedback only if you are ready to change

How often have you been asked to participate in a survey and never heard about it again? How often do companies run surveys and file the results in oblivion? Often enough to leave the impression on customers that surveys are a waste of time. If that is the case, surveys become a very frustrating experience for the customers and a waste of money for the enterprise. This is why we emphasise that before asking for feedback, the enterprise should be ready and willing to apply the learning. In quality circles this is called going the full PDCA loop: Plan, Do, Check, Act – from plan to change.

Set the right expectations

If you ask for customer feedback, it does not mean that you have to implement or change everything customers ask for. However, when introducing a survey you should set the right expectations: explain why you conduct the survey and what you plan to do with the results. And at the end, communicate the results and your action: 'We asked. . . You told us. . . We acted. . .'

Ask few, relevant questions

One of the key success factors for a survey is to limit it to really relevant questions. There is only so much learning and change an organisation can handle at one time. Learn a few important lessons, improve and then move on to the next ones. If customers experience over time that the enterprise is serious about their feedback, they will continue to give feedback. Within their one-to-one marketing concept, Don Peppers and Martha Rogers call this the learning experience. Electronic media like the Web and e-mail offer an excellent platform for the learning experience.

Questions from customers are messages

Whenever customers ask questions whose answers ought to be found somewhere in the supplier's web site, the additional message they are also sending is: 'This is not clear', 'I cannot find', 'Your information is incomplete'. The usual procedure by the supplier then is: open a case, log the question, find the answer and close the case. In a customer-centric enterprise the case is not closed yet: the questions and answers are forwarded to an appropriate department, sometimes the quality department, that undertakes to find out what could be improved to prevent the same questions from occurring in the future.

For example, if the customer could not find specific information on the Web and sends an e-mail to the webmaster, it could be an indication that the information is not published on the Web, or that the navigation leading to the information is not clear. If a customer dials a call centre for help on a recently purchased product, it could be an indication that the self-help service feature does not list the problem and the answers yet, or that the key words the customer used are not set up in the service search engine. Again, by using a quality approach to analyse the incidents and correct the underlying cause, the enterprise can improve the quality of service. This will lead to two positive changes: (a) customers will be able to serve themselves and get answers quickly; and (b) the workload on the support department is reduced.

Benefits for your customers:

- Customers can always and easily send you questions, comments, complaints or praise whenever it is convenient for them to do so.
- Forms pre-filled with customer and context-sensitive data ease the feedback process for the customer.
- Answering surveys is a positive experience for customers and leads to improvements, with corresponding benefits in the area surveyed.

Benefits for your enterprise:

- Every customer feedback item or question is an opportunity to serve and to sell.
- Pre-filled forms increase the likelihood that customers will use them.
- Acquired customer knowledge that is made available throughout the enterprise improves the quality of decisions and results in more competitive, customer-focused products and services.

Harnessing the power of customer information

The dream, if not the goal, of many marketing managers is to have access to enough good customer information to be able to segment the customer base according to different criteria, to design focused campaigns and promotions that generate profitable sales and to build tailored content and messages that improve the quality of their customer relationship programmes. In order to gain such information, customer data must be gathered from multiple sources, such as front-end web applications and back-end systems, and consolidated into a common information store application that offers a consolidated, 360-degree view of the customer. This is in fact the role of customer information management (CIM) processes that, in addition to gathering and consolidating customer information, must also maintain it to keep it current.

The store application may be called a data warehouse, a data mart or an information store, depending on the selected vendor. For the purpose of this chapter we will call it the consolidated customer data store (CCDS). The basic principle is known: CIM processes extract customer data from multiple businesses and transactional applications, both back end and front end, aggregate them and store them in one database. This database (CCDS) is built and optimised for the main purpose of querying and analysing the data.

Once the CCDS is populated with enough customer data, you have the possibility of gaining new insights into customers' purchase behaviours and patterns, you can discover what products or content your main target groups prefer, you can determine how successful certain campaigns were and so on. All of these ultimately lead to more effective marketing.

Out of the many benefits and insights that a CCDS offers, let's consider a few related to an e-CRM scenario (see Figure 6.3):

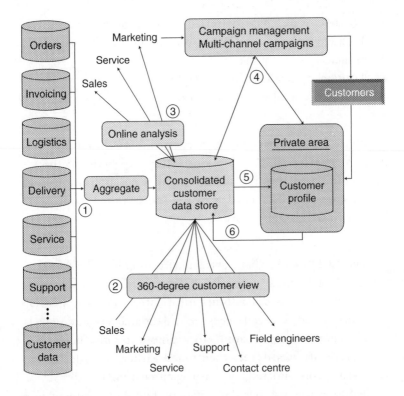

Figure 6.3: An integrated, consolidated customer data store enables customer-oriented sales, marketing and service

- To gather customer information from different enterprise processes and databases.
- To build a 360-degree view of the customer that can be made available to all customer-facing departments in the enterprise.
- To provide online analysis of customer information to enhance campaign management and sharpen the order-generation process to enrich customer profiles.
- To develop more sophisticated customer segmentation and target group definitions.

- To analyse purchase patterns and customer profitability.
- To analyse customers' Web, e-mail and other channel usage.
- To gain deeper customer insights in order to improve Web and e-mail personalisation.

Figure 6.3 also illustrates an integrated, closed-loop marketing system where the CCDS closes the loop between the actions initiated through the front-end web applications and the business results recorded in the transactional databases. This is how it would work:

1 The CCDS stores data extracted from enterprise transactional back-end systems, from the web front end and other external sources of customer information. Because a CCDS is optimised for read access and data analysis, the data is aggregated before loading to enable fast and efficient analysis afterwards. As mentioned earlier, in order to reach a consolidated view for each customer and deduplicate customer data, it is preferable to implement a unique customer ID for all individual customer data coming from multiple sources.

2 Any department with customer contact can obtain a customised view of the customer data that is relevant to their customer-oriented activity. If the CCDS receives data from all customer touch points, the 360-degree view of the customer provides the background information needed for all future customer contacts: before visiting the customer, the sales rep can learn if there are any outstanding customer service issues; the new field engineer can see what products the customer has installed and their repair history; the marketing rep can see what promotion campaigns the customer responded to, just to name a few examples.

3 Analytical tools are available to slice and dice data in multiple ways: to segment customers according to specific parameters (product category, recency of purchase etc.) or to build clusters of people with similar purchasing patterns. Online analytical processing (OLAP) tools allow users to perform complex queries and to drill down into details. Data-mining tools can go through large sets of data to uncover hidden patterns and identify new clusters of customers. These tools can assist your decision-making process both at the strategic level (marketing investment decisions) and at the tactical level (campaign design).

4 You have the opportunity to develop a closed-loop marketing campaign: you address a previously defined target group and decide what content they will receive, and you decide through which channel (Web or e-mail) they will receive the content and which results you want to track and feed back into the CCDS for further analysis. If you plan a promotional e-mail campaign, by integrating CCDS with an e-mail marketing solution you create a list of addresses – which, of course, includes only customers who have agreed to receive e-mail campaigns – that is fed directly into the e-mail engine.

5 Over time with this architecture you can refine customer profiles so that they better represent the individual customer's attitude and needs. As an example, you would be able to classify your customers as frequent buyers or occasional buyers; as early adopters or followers; as experienced users or beginners. When this information is added to the customer profile in the private area, you can better customise the content to which the customer has access. Earlier in the book we referred to this classification as the 'hidden profile' because it cannot be checked or updated by customers themselves. Hidden profile attributes are derived from analysis and interpretation of the

customer data. Interpretation can lead to errors, therefore a great deal of caution must be exercised when developing a hidden profile. CIM has a very important role in this scenario, which is to keep the customer profile up to date; otherwise you cannot address the right messages, content and services to the right customers.

6   To close the loop, data related to the customer profile and to Web activity measurements are fed back into the CCDS for further evaluation. While it is conceivable to store all sorts of interesting facts about customer behaviour, there are two important things to consider: (a) CIM costs grow with the number of records stored, so keep in the CCDS only the data that you know how to use and that you intend to use in the future; (b) data obtained through the observation of customer behaviour and later stored is also subject to data privacy legislation. It is recommended that you ask the customer's permission to observe and store individual Web activity data in order to improve the online customer experience, the products offered and so on.

In most cases much of the relevant data for populating a CCDS already exists in separate back-end or front-end systems. The challenge is to extract, consolidate and import the data into a CCDS. While this is not a trivial IT problem, it is mainly a CIM problem because common processes and conventions (such as the unique customer identifier) need to be applied to all customer data sources for acquiring, storing and maintaining customer information. The value of a CCDS is directly related to the quality of the information stored within it. Once set up, the CCDS needs a feeding and maintenance process that imports and maintains quality data. To build a CCDS is both an IT and a CIM challenge, but the benefits gained in terms of customer knowledge, improved customer relationships and business results are worth the investment.

Benefits for your customers:

- Ultimately, customers will benefit in terms of improved customer service from enhanced personalisation and better-targeted content.

Benefits for your enterprise:

- A better-informed and customer-centred decision-making process, thanks to a robust customer information management and analysis capability.
- An integrated solution that supports more efficient customer relationship management and more effective campaign management.
- Closed-loop marketing and campaign management lead to increased sales.
- A 360-degree view of the customer leads to improved customer service.
- Customer information management and analysis processes enable a learning relationship.

Co-existence with the distribution channel

If you do not serve your end-customers directly but via a distribution channel, your Web or e-mail communications with end-users may meet with opposition from that channel, who may think you are trying to steal 'their customers'. However, as we said on page 34, your one-to-one communication with end-user customers need not disrupt the relationship they have with the channel, it may instead increase their business through that channel.

First, you must have a clear channel strategy for your business model. It is the business model that determines the

Table 6.1: Many options are available for integrating e-CRM with distribution channels, benefiting both the manufacturer and the channnels

Enterprise web site feature	Dealer involvement
Link to the dealer's web site.	Dealer builds and maintains web site independently. This is the lowest level of co-existence.
Dealer locator: customers can locate dealers best fitting their needs (distance, products available, service offered); could show address text only or accompanied by maps.	Dealer provides content used as selection criteria.
Request for contact or service call: forwarded to dealer (request sales rep visit; request phone call; request maintenance).	Dealer responds to customer request (contacts the customer, proposal for alternative date/time, confirmation).
Customer profile set to receive news from one or more specific dealers. Customer receives news on the Web or via e-mails.	Dealer provides news content, runs promotions on stocked items.
Online ordering with drop shipment at closest dealer premises. Customer orders items online and picks them up at the dealer's shop.	Dealer delivers equipment (for which receives commission) and offers after-sales services to customer (installation support, upgrade services etc.).

distribution strategy and the choice of electronic communication tools, not the other way around, otherwise you will
have channel conflict.

You can certainly design your e-CRM strategy to sell
direct, but you can also design it to support your current
distribution channels. In the latter case your one-to-one
communications co-exist with and reinforce your channels'
relationships with end-users.

Table 6.1 gives some examples of how an enterprise web
site featuring personalised end-user services could co-exist
with a dealer or retail channel, with the objective of
increasing its business with its customers. In all these
examples, the enterprise provides a central infrastructure,
processes and resources for one-to-one communications with
end-users. Distribution channels provide mainly content and
services. Although dealers and retailers can and do establish

their own web sites, they are not likely to make the investments needed for a sophisticated, personalised communication environment – they do not have the same interest as you in building up your brand. However, to accept the business model whereby your brand maintains one-to-one communication with consumers, they must hear and believe that the objective is to drive customer traffic and business to them.

Before adopting a strategy of co-existence at a certain level, it is very important to gain a clear commitment from your channel that it will actively participate and contribute the requested value. If your channel does not contribute the content and services as needed when needed, it could even harm your business. Therefore it is wise to formalise such collaboration through a *Service-level agreement* that covers the following:

- *Your tasks.* To provide and maintain the infrastructure, processes and resources to run a personalised electronic environment for end-user customers, also covering services such as a call centre if applicable. As an additional service you could offer to provide reports so that your channel is informed about customer profiles, about e-mail or web campaign results and about customer ratings of the quality of service provided.
- *Your dealers' tasks.* To provide your web site regularly with up-to-date content. To fulfil customer services as offered in the web site. To meet your privacy statement guidelines. To send promotions only to customers who profiled accordingly. To promote the enterprise web site to customers of your brand.

These are only examples of the sort of action required to co-exist effectively with the distribution channels when engaging in e-marketing.

Benefits for your customers:

- They are not confused by separate and competing e-marketing strategies from the enterprise and its dealers.
- They get the best service through the integration of enterprise and dealer services.

Benefits for your enterprise:

- You manage the total customer experience, increase customer satisfaction and maintain customer loyalty.
- Your dealers are aware that you know the end-customers as well if not better than they do. This will motivate them to co-operate in e-marketing initiatives.
- Dealers that accept and work in this mode show more loyalty to your brand.

Benefits for your dealers:

- They do not have to build web sites with e-CRM features, but can leverage the capability of the enterprise's web site.
- They can earn additional dealer service revenues and profits by serving their and your customers through your web site.

Dealing with real people

CHAPTER 7

Overview

In this chapter we find that:

- Customers are neither computer sessions nor mouse clicks – they are real people with feelings and emotions.
- Localisation is more than language translation.
- Customer privacy matters and companies should meet their customers' concerns in this respect.

E-psychology

Until now we have been talking about dynamic web sites, automated e-mail, context-sensitive feedback, Web to back-end integration – where does psychology fit in?

First, let us reassure you: e-psychology is not, at least not yet, a Web-based application for human–machine interaction. We use the term e-psychology to remind ourselves that any e-CRM architecture or application is not there to serve other software machines but real people with expectations, emotions and feelings. E-psychology is not a new body of knowledge but a set of known communication practices that address human behaviour through electronic media. It is about acting in a virtual environment, as you would act in a real, person-to-person environment.

Managing expectations

It is so easy to ask questions or make announcements, but before you do so, think about the expectations you may raise. If you ask for a customers' birthday, they may think they will receive a birthday card at the appropriate

> **KEY CONCEPT**
>
> Every question you ask your customers, every piece of information you send, every announcement you make sets an expectation.

time. If you send a registration form, your customer will expect you to use only the address entered in the form – no other address should be used from then on. If you announce a new service, your customer will expect to be entitled to it. The same as with any form of communication, you should try to interpret the message or question from the recipients' viewpoint before sending it.

Personalise only to a level acceptable to the customer

Some customers like personalisation, some do not. Some customers like recommendations based on observations, some do not. The higher the personalisation level you offer, the higher the risk that your customers feel you are invading their privacy. Relationships evolve over time. An advanced personalisation engine may serve your long-time and loyal customers well, but perhaps you should not use the same personalisation rules and implied customer intimacy with first-time buyers. You don't know them yet and they don't know you.

Welcome, thank and apologise when appropriate

By now it should be clear that the Web and e-mail are also communication channels. To decide what expressions to use or what feeling to transmit, just transfer the situation into a real-life setting. If a customer has given you new information that helps you improve your service, thank them. If a customer has entered your shop but your shop is closed, apologise: 'We are sorry we cannot serve you now, our shop is currently unavailable' instead of 'We cannot serve you now, our shop is currently unavailable'. The difference is one word, but customers feel as if they are being treated like human beings rather than unwanted events.

The important thought is this: for a customer there is no difference between experiencing a situation with you as a person on the other side of a desk or with you as a web page on the other side of cyberspace. The *feelings* are the same: the customer can be indifferent, disappointed, annoyed or delighted with the experience. The challenge in process and system design is to think ahead of the events that could happen and the situations that could develop and to decide how to communicate and act as a consequence. If you anticipate your customers' feelings and respond to them accordingly, your customers will feel well treated even if the interaction takes place in an automated web or e-mail environment.

In her book *Customers.com*, Patricia Seybold describes this as 'offer peace of mind'. Some customers will not care about the 'sorry', but it does not harm. However, for the customers who care the 'sorry' changes the customer perception and improves the customer experience, although the facts have not changed. So why not say it and other words like it?

- *Sorry* for this unexpected delay. Please find here. . .
- *Welcome* to our monthly newsletter.

- *Thanks* for completing the profile.
- *Thank you* so much for your order.
- We truly *appreciate* your patience.

Acknowledge requests and confirm action

Web applications are automated tools and, as everybody knows, automated tools can fail. After a customer has ordered an item on your web site, has requested a service call or some specific information, they could wonder whether the web site has processed their request correctly and when they will get a response. First, acknowledge that you have received the request. Second, let the customer know what the next step is and when it will happen: 'We will ship your order tomorrow', 'Our service agent will work on your service request in the next two hours'. This is to reassure the customer that everything is in order and that the request is being processed. This is especially important if the customer is new to your enterprise and doesn't know your procedures.

Keep the customer informed about what is going on – if you cannot deliver what you promised, offer alternatives

A customer orders an item marked 'next-day delivery'. The supplier acknowledges and confirms the order by return e-mail. The item goes out of stock before the order can be fulfilled. The back-end system starts the procedure for restocking the item and waits for confirmation from the vendor before updating delivery information. In this scenario, the customer receives no communication about what is going on. What are the customer's thoughts when the expected item does not arrive? 'Why haven't they sent it? Did they process the order correctly? Will they charge me anyway? When will I finally get it? The enterprise should not let the customer dwell too long with negative thoughts. As soon as the out-of-stock notification goes out, a message could be sent to the customer:

Dear Mr Customer. We are very sorry for not shipping your order no. XYZ as promised. The item ran out of stock before we could fulfil the order. We expect to ship the item to you within 10 days from now and will send you a confirmation as soon as we receive the item from the vendor. Of course, we will charge your credit card only after you receive the shipment. If because of this delay you prefer to cancel the order please follow this link: <link>. We apologise for the inconvenience and hope to serve you again in the future.

You may question why you should offer a link to cancel the order. If the customer really wants to cancel the order, they will do so in any case. If you do not offer such a link or another easy cancellation procedure, the customer will eventually find a way to cancel the order, but it will require more effort and create negative emotions. If you offer the link, of course you make it easy for the customer to cancel, but the customer will not feel trapped and will remember how easy it is to do business with you, which are both positive experiences for developing the right customer relationship and for future business. And, more likely than not, the customer will wait for the shipment to occur.

The bottom line is that if you made a commitment you cannot meet you must notify the customer of what has changed and, if appropriate, offer them an alternative solution.

Classify customers without creating class problems

If you offer premium services to specific customers (your most important, most valued, most profitable customers), it is wise to make sure that customers who are not entitled to receive premium services do not feel that they are treated like second-class citizens. If they are aware of the premium services, they should know the entitlement criteria and how they can reach the next level of customer service. In addition, the Web can help you offer premium services to specific customers without other customers noticing it. If you run a personalised web site and offer a private area, every individual customer receives exactly the information and services targeted to their level of personalisation and they will all feel treated well.

The downside of personalisation

Personalisation could also have a downside. Customers like to specify what content they want to see in their personalised web site, but at the same time can be afraid that this feature will make them miss 'important information'. To avoid this fear, offer your customers the possibility of switching from the personalised view to a show-me-all view that displays all the content publicly available on your site.

Have something new to say

This is not a new topic. Earlier we said that content and dialogue are at the basis of customer relationship management. Nevertheless, how many web sites do you know that offer the same content (especially on the home page) for weeks or even months?

Imagine the following situation: you meet a business partner today and tell him a customer story. The business partner finds the story interesting. Next week you invite the business partner for lunch because you have a story to tell. You meet and you tell him the same story again. Although the story is still interesting, your business partner wonders why you're telling him again. You meet again the following week and once more you tell him the same story. This time your business partner will ask himself if you are losing your memory or think he has lost his. He will probably avoid you from now on.

The bottom line is that dialogue without content doesn't last long. Keep your web site up to date, publish fresh information on a regular basis and let your customers find gold in your site – then they will be motivated to come back and visit your site again.

Passwords procedures

Don't forget the 'forgot my password' problem. Many people occasionally forget their passwords, not because of poor memory, but because there are so many codes and passwords to remember and not all of them are used frequently enough to remember.

Last month your customer specified a user ID and password. Today she wants to return to your site, she enters the user ID and asks, 'What was my password?' That is a function you should offer on your site. If you want your customers to come back to your web site again, you ought to offer an easy and secure way for them to get back their password.

There are some procedures that have proved to work well, including the following two:

- A 'Send me my password' button: the user clicks on the button and your e-CRM web application automatically sends the customer's password to their e-mail address. Advantage: easy and reasonably secure process. Disadvantage: some people do not like the fact that companies can look up their passwords.

- A 'Send me a password' button: the user clicks on the button and your e-CRM web application automatically creates a new password and sends it to the customer's e-mail address. Advantage: no conflict with customers who don't want you to look up their password. Disadvantage: customer has to change the password after entering the web site.

Sending a password via e-mail is considered reasonably secure because you can assume that the customer has secured their e-mail access by password and that no one else has access to their e-mail account.

Give helpful error messages

This is another very basic subject. Although it seems obvious that error messages should be helpful, many web sites today seem to ignore this subject. Error messages are by their nature annoying and unintelligible error messages are even more so. There is a very simple approach for creating clear and precise error messages that are helpful: don't tell the visitor that *something* is wrong, but *what* is wrong (see Table 7.1).

Most error messages are not thought about from the customer's perspective but from a systems perspective and customers are very seldom involved during test procedures. Unclear error messages are annoying and at times frustrating, because the customer has to guess what is wrong and sometimes is unable to do so. All this is a waste of time, the one currency the customer is short of. Why make it hard for

Table 7.1: Only precise error messages support the user

Instead of	Show
A required field is empty.	Please specify the order quantity.
Invalid date.	Please enter the date in the format day/month/year.

the customer to enter the correct data? Spend some time and check out the error messages on your web site and see if you can easily understand them.

Localisation

As we said at the beginning of the book, multilingual and multicultural issues are

> ## KEY CONCEPT
>
> In the e-world, people communicate and do business through hardware and software machines and through black boxes and networks. System designers may forget that behind all this there are users who display human behaviour and emotions. By designing web processes that deal with real people rather than pages or clicks, you strengthen your customers' positive feelings, avoid anger or fear and can constructively respond to negative feelings. Your customer relationships will be made stronger as a result.

likely to affect the penetration of the Internet throughout the non-English speaking world. After the very fast ramp-up phase, these issues represent an opportunity for Internet service providers and content providers who service national or regional audiences to gain additional market share, either through local-language editions of their global services or through dedicated national or regional services. Enterprises that do business on a global basis regularly deal with multilingual and multicultural issues within their business and communication strategies. Translation and localisation of content have long been part and parcel of marketing communications budgets for traditional media in global enterprises, even though such budgets have often been hotly debated.

However, the global reach of the Web, the widespread use of English (in some form or other) and the possibility of creating content once, in one place, for instant worldwide publication may give the illusion that these issues can now be short-circuited. In the context of CRM we believe, on the contrary, that the personalisation features offered by the Web will create even bigger demands for careful translation, adaptation and localisation of content into national and regional cultural and linguistic environments. In this section we present some subjects to consider.

Language

If your web site offers content in English or, more generally, in one specific language, you may automatically exclude from your web site everyone who is not conversant with the language you offer. Of course, more and more people read English at some level of proficiency, particularly in the technology and business world, but even then many people will not entirely understand the English text on the Web or will interpret it wrongly because they miss the cultural and linguistic context. The web site will not offer the intended value to those visitors and may even be counter-productive if it raises questions that are left unanswered.

In addition, there are countries that have such a strong bond to their native language (for example France) that even people who have a fair knowledge of the language would not visit an English-only web site. Localisation may be less of a critical issue in an international business-to-business environment, where English is usually not a problem, than in a business-to-consumer environment, but in either case you cannot overlook it.

Salutation

'Hello Susan, Hello John' – how often do you see this? How many people think that being greeted by their first name is OK? Probably quite a few. How many people think it's not OK? Probably as many. Many e-marketers think that by greeting visitors or customers by their first name, on the web home page or in an e-mail, they have taken a giant step towards personalisation and customer intimacy. Being greeted by your first name by a stranger through a surrogate electronic medium may be acceptable in some countries and in some socio-economic environments, but is not accepted everywhere. There are countries in Europe and Asia (such as Austria, the Netherlands, Belgium and Japan) where being greeted by their first name puts people off. Different countries have different cultures. In some, people want to be greeted by their last name or by their title followed by their last name. If you greet them by their first name they may feel offended.

Salutations are very country specific. In Japan you do not just use the person's name, you add a 'san' suffix to the name to obtain a polite form of a greeting. Salutation by title and name are different in Austria and Germany, although both countries have German as their language. Therefore personalisation means much more than greeting by first name. A truly personalised e-mail or web site would include a salutation that respects the conventions of the countries addressed. It may seem a small and unimportant thing, but it can open a world of difference between you and your competitors. A country's culture does not vanish in the Web.

Registration fields

Registration forms are not rocket science, which is possibly why many companies don't think of them as an important component of their CRM strategy. Say that you are a non-US visitor trying to register in a site designed in the US. Within the mandatory fields you find 'State' and 'Zip code'. It is no use trying to work around them, you will not be allowed to register and entering false information won't get you the necessary information anyway. The issue here is not only that visitors cannot register to obtain the requested service; it is that visitors from countries outside the US receive the impression that the web site is US focused and does not serve global customers. Even if that is the strategy for the specific web site, all it takes is the inclusion of a pull-down menu with a list of all countries, with links to other pages that explain what services are available and how to receive them.

Or take the case of a field that accepts telephone numbers only in the ooo—ooooooo format. Phone number schemes are different from region to region, so asking visitors to enter data in a non-compatible format could confuse them and cause them to leave the site without having registered. Offering a 0800 number is fine as long as the visitors are in the country where the free phone service is operational; if you try to call that number from outside the country the most likely outcome is an automatic answer saying that the number is not valid. This can be especially frustrating if you try to reach customer service because you have a problem and need help and you have no alternative number. Again, it is not a question of technology – you can provide a full international number as back-up or a list of local 800 numbers that forward the calls to your central service center. It's just a question of thinking of customers first and beyond the boundaries of the local environment. Think global and act local.

Time conventions and units of measurement

While for an experienced traveller '10am PST', '1pm EST', and '1900 CET' mean the same time, many people do not know what the acronyms mean and cannot relate time zones to longitude without a map. What does this have to do with personalisation? Personalisation also means publishing local time data for all the countries where the service is offered. If you announce a webcast for 9 am PST, you could miss many potential viewers if at the same time you don't publish the equivalent time for all the time zones you intend to reach. If your web site services make use of weight, volume, temperature, distance or whatever unit of measure, make sure the information is represented in both metric and equivalent British or American measures. Not everyone knows that 1 litre equals 35.211 fluid ounces.

Prices, currencies and taxes

If you intend to publish list prices or suggested retail prices on your web site, what issues do you face? Let's set aside the issues of pricing policies and mark-ups in different countries around the world, not because they are unimportant, but because they are company specific and should be dealt with elsewhere. Before publishing prices on the Web, consult with your legal and tax departments. Prices should preferably be published in the customer's local currency, which means that you assume the foreign exchange risk. This risk diminishes if you operate within a trading bloc where exchange rates among member countries tend to be stable and, of course, it disappears if you only do business, say, in the US in US dollars, or in eurozone countries in euros.

The euro is now a major trading bloc currency and will also become compulsory for retail transactions within and across eurozone countries in 2002, so products or services addressed to customers within the eurozone should be priced in euros. However, the euro is not yet well understood by consumers. It will take time for Europeans, even in eurozone countries, to become accustomed to the euro, even though euro prices are already posted next to local-currency prices and the exchange rate between the US dollar and the euro is widely publicised in the media. The conversion rates between eurozone currencies and the euro are fixed, but they are awkward numbers to remember, with lots of digits – who can remember that one euro is 6.55957 French francs or 0.787564 Irish punts?

If you are offering a product or service in eurozone countries, it may be advisable to include a pull-down conversion calculator feature next to the euro price. This way, customers from, say, Spain can figure out how many pesetas it costs and relate the price to their previous market experience. It may make the European Commission frown, but it may give you a competitive advantage.

Taxes are the most innovative product of governments. Value added tax, purchase tax, governor's tax and others are levied on commercial transactions in most parts of the world. E-business transactions across countries may also fall victim to governments' tax creativity in the future. When you publish local prices you need to indicate whether they include local taxes or not. Prices are sometimes published without VAT in business-to-business transactions where VAT is recoverable through tax reporting. Again, check with your legal and tax departments.

Product and service availability

If, for whatever reason, an enterprise does not sell all of its products and services in all countries, it must take on the responsibility of making it easy for web site visitors to find out what products and services are available in their countries. It is very frustrating for a consumer who has read all the product information and wants to purchase the product to find out from the local distribution or retail network that it does not carry that product, or after enquiring at the manufacturer to hear, 'Sorry, we do not sell this product in your country'.

The product web page should clearly describe in what countries the product is *not* available, and the personalised web site for those countries should not display unavailable products because, by definition, they do not meet the customer profile.

E-PRIVACY **181**

Benefits for your customers:

- They receive products and services that meet the linguistic and cultural needs of their environment.
- They do not have to spend time and resources to translate or interpret information so that it makes sense to them.

Benefits for your enterprise:

- You will not lose prospects due to misunderstandings.
- You increase customer satisfaction by using conventions and expressions with which they are familiar.
- You will gain competitive advantage if you consistently localise your products, services and customer communications.

E-privacy

It's Saturday. You take your car and drive to a department store that you have not previously visited. At the entrance, a guide asks you to type your name into a data-entry device. In exchange you get a gizmo to wear on you for as long as you stay in the store. You ask why. You learn that this way the retailer can trace every step you take in the store. When you come out of the store, it will be able to describe exactly what itinerary you followed through the store, what displays you looked at, what products you took into your hands and put down again, what you bought and to whom you talked. Not only that, but the next time you visit the same store it will still remember all that. In addition to the gizmo, you will be handed a suggested list of goods to purchase and instructions on where to find them. Would you like this?

In the world of bricks-and-mortar department stores, this is still an improbable scenario. In the world of e-shopping, web site owners and web store owners think that this scenario is perfectly normal and doable: 'This is just the Web – of course we can do it.' Their motivation may be legitimate: because business on the Web is conducted in a non-personal way, often the only way to personalise the customer experience and offer better service is to track the customer's presence and activity on the Web and to acquire and use the customer's data. After all, most customers like to be recognised, to be greeted by name and to have their preferences remembered by those businesses to which they give their custom – that is the sort of personalised experience that small shops and boutiques gave their clientele before the era of shopping malls and hypermarkets.

However, do e-shoppers know what events are monitored, what information is collected about them and stored or how it is used? And if they do know about it, do they agree to it? And if they do not agree to it, do they know what to do? In short: how do they know if you respect their privacy?

Customers are concerned about the way companies use and protect their personal data. They care about their privacy – and so should you. To show that they do care, companies have developed privacy policies. These are a prerequisite for building electronic relationships with customers and for giving customers confidence to release data to the companies they do business with.

The privacy statement published on your web site essentially displays your privacy policy to your customers. It discloses all the relevant facts about how your organisation uses and protects customers' data. It should be easy to read, it should list all relevant privacy policy components and it should be posted on your web site so that it is easy to find with one click – preferably from every page.

The main subject of the privacy policy is all the data that is collected online and that can be used to identify a customer uniquely. The data is either released to you by an individual customer or tracked and logged by you without active customer participation. An expression quite often used to describe this is 'personally identifiable information'.

 IMPLEMENTATION CHECKLIST: Privacy policies

A privacy policy can cover many topics. We suggest that you cover at least the following, which we view as most important.

- The type of data collected and for what purpose. Typical reasons would include improving customer service; improving products; order fulfilment or billing; providing better web content; contacting the customer for marketing purposes. It would be appropriate to outline the benefits that customers receive from the uses of their data.
- The methods used to collect the data, such as self-registration, cookies or clickstream logs. A short and clear explanation of the method used is a must. If you use cookies, you should also inform users that they can refuse the cookie and how this affects their Web session.
- The channels used to track information, such as the Web, e-mail, WAP, SMS, fax. Your privacy policy should reflect all the channels used by your e-marketing strategy, not just the Web. For example, if you send personalised e-mail with embedded links that can be tracked down to the individual, this method must be stated in the policy. This type of e-mail should also include a link to the privacy statement on your website.
- The measures available to the customer to prevent the enterprise from collecting certain data or from using the

data for certain purposes. Appropriate features on the Web should be offered as well as an e-mail address, phone or fax number or postal address where the customer can get help. The main objective is to make it as easy as possible for customers to determine what you are allowed to do with their data.

- Whether your enterprise releases customer data to subsidiaries, partners, dealers or other third parties and for what reason.

- The fact that you *do not* sell or rent customer data to external companies.

- How customers can have access to their personal data and have it updated or corrected. Again, a web feature should be made available backed up by an e-mail address and/or phone number, fax number or postal address.

- If your enterprise does not collect data, the privacy statement should mention this.

- Different methods, if any, for collecting data in the public part of your site and in the private area. For example, in the public part you use cookies while in the private area you log clickstreams for personalisation purposes.

- Commitment to child privacy. This is a hot topic and subject to stringent legal requirements. In the US a new law, the Children's OnLine Privacy Protection Act, is aimed especially at sites that collect personal data from children under 13 years of age. If you target your web site or parts of it at children or knowingly collect personal data from children, the privacy statement should clearly describe how you comply with child privacy laws in the countries you address. In addition to all other items listed above, at a minimum your web site should obtain explicit parental approval to collect data, have a process that records and maintains that approval and give access to parents to change or delete their children's data.

◆ The method used by your enterprise to ensure data security so that only authenticated and authorised people can access it.

Customer data privacy is a rapidly evolving subject. In 1998 the European Commission published a directive on data privacy that prohibits the transfer of personal data to non-European Union nations that do not meet the European 'adequacy' standard for privacy protection. In 2000 the EU and the US agreed on a 'safe harbour' framework for privacy protection that allows US companies that certify to the 'safe harbour' provisions to continue business dealings with EU companies without interruption of their data flows. More developments can be expected, so it is important to keep up to date.

To gain more insights on privacy issues, you may wish to visit www.bbbonline.com, www.truste.com or www.export. gov/safeharbor/.

There are some other important aspects of the privacy policy that you need to consider:

■ Every employee in the enterprise must abide by the privacy policy, without exception. There is no working around the privacy policy; that is simply prohibited. The policy could be suspended under certain circumstances for a specific and limited time, but the customers affected would have to give their permission first.

■ If you change your data-collection method in such a way that customer privacy is affected, then you must update your policy and send it to customers, pointing to the changes. For example, if you switch your e-mail marketing system from non-personalised to personalised e-mails with embedded traceable links, add this change to your privacy policy and inform your customers about it. Of course, you must at the same time give your customers the option of declining the new e-mail methodology.

■ Similarly, if you decide to use existing customer data in a way that is different from what you disclosed in your privacy statement, you must inform your customers about your plans and explain how they can accept or decline.

There are two ways of asking customers' approval to changes in the privacy statement. *Active* approval asks the individual customer for explicit permission to change or suspend the privacy policy for a specific topic. *Passive* approval informs customers about the change and informs them how to decline if they do not accept the change.

We recommend that you adopt the active approval. Although passive approval is the easier and faster way to introduce a change in the policy and is the preferred method for many companies, it does not serve relationship marketing well.

In his book *Permission Marketing*, Seth Godin explains that permission (obtained from an individual customer for a specific topic, such as promotional e-mail) is not transferable. We think that this principle should be applied to the privacy policy as well. If the information about the planned policy change does not reach your customer or is not read for whatever reason, how can anyone assume that the customer agreed to the change?

Active approval builds trust. Of course, you should make it easy for the customer to give approval (through a web site feature, phone number, fax number or pre-paid postal return letter).

Designing and implementing a privacy policy takes time and effort, but the outcome is greater trust, which leads to a higher degree of customer intimacy. Promote the privacy statement. Let your customers know you are serious about protecting their data privacy.

Benefits for your customers:

- They know precisely how you use their personal data and how you protect their privacy.
- They know how to have access and exercise control over their personal data.

Benefits for your enterprise:

- A privacy policy will help you understand the boundaries of your overall e-marketing environment and design professional marketing programmes.
- By stating and observing a clear and robust privacy policy, you build a foundation for lasting customer relationships based on trust.

Getting it done

CHAPTER 8

Overview

This chapter proposes a set of steps as guidelines for successful e-CRM project implementation:

- Key steps you should take.
- Whom to bring in, whom to get support from, whom to support.
- Key project phases and what customers need to tell you.

By now you will be convinced that the most effective role for e-marketing is to build and maintain long-lasting customer relationships in the e-world. You will also understand the concept of e-CRM, the practice of managing customer relationships through electronic media. The scenarios we have presented and the recommendations we have made will have motivated you to want to start trying it. Now you need to know what it takes to make it happen, where you start, what steps you take and how you know you've finished.

The answers, of course, depend a great deal on your individual business situation and your current experience with customer relationship management and with marketing on the Web. While it is clearly not possible to give a comprehensive step-by-step approach that covers all possible situations, we hope that this chapter will be beneficial in providing a useful framework for implementing e-CRM within your enterprise. We will not cover topics specific to IT (hardware and software infrastructure, database solutions, web applications, front-end and back-end integration and the like). Our recommendation is that you involve your IT people from the very beginning to contribute to all of the IT aspects of the project, including the selection of vendors of solutions and services. Here we cover the most important phases and steps of the implementation – those that can lead to project success or failure. The order in which we cover the subject is also not cast in stone: depending on your business environment, experience, goals, existing tools and processes, some steps could be skipped, run in parallel or in a different sequence.

Remember that e-CRM, in this context, covers the *relationship* part of the total customer experience, not the *product* side of the experience. For example, advanced customisation of products and services is not considered here and would require additional steps.

Vision, mission and plan

Too many projects fail because people plunge right away into the plan and its execution without understanding the higher-order purpose of the project. All major project decisions should be tested to see if they support that purpose. If they don't, the danger is that the project will take on a life of its own and, even if well executed, will not provide the expected return on investment. You need a vision statement and a mission statement to communicate the higher-order purpose.

The vision is a vivid description of that higher-order purpose. It is a picture and/or a set of statements that describe the experience of the targeted recipients or users of final outcome of the project. In the case of e-CRM, the vision would give a picture or a feel of the desired customer experience through the electronic media made available to customers. If the vision is expressed in words, it is best expressed in the words of the customers themselves. For example:

- When I visit the site I am always recognised wherever I go.
- They remember and respect my preferences for information and the way it should be presented.
- Concise e-mail messages alert me to significant new developments and opportunities in my field of interest.
- I never receive unsolicited mail.
- My comments and questions are always acknowledged and answered in a courteous and competent way.

While it is always a good exercise to ask customers about their expectations before working on a vision for the project, it is even more important to test the vision with customers after formulating it. Let customers tell you if they are excited about what you are trying to build and how they rank it compared to your competitors.

The mission is the organisational objective to deliver the desired experiences to customers in a way that meets or even exceeds their expectations and that differentiates the enterprise from its competitors. In other words, the mission is the value proposition of the e-CRM project. And the plan, of course, is the description of the implementation steps organised by priority.

Why spend time on a vision? Because an e-CRM project needs not just the intellectual assent, but the active co-operation and involvement of all the customer-facing departments and employees in the enterprise. Unless they have the same mental picture of the desired outcome and unless they take ownership of their part of the plan to serve customers better, the e-CRM project will not deliver the desired results.

Secure management commitment

E-CRM is not just a technology project, but also a 'change project' that alters the way and the perspective on how things are done in the area of customer relations. For the project to be successful, it is extremely important to secure high-level management commitment for the entire life of the project. Because it is a change project, there will be gaps to fill, inhibiting factors to overcome and supporting factors to highlight.

There is always resistance to change and that is where management will be needed to help steer the project so that it doesn't run aground. And there is always the question of commitment to project funding, which can only come from upper management.

Involve all customer-facing departments

As we have already said, all entities in direct customer contact should participate in the e-CRM programme from the beginning. CRM should not be perceived as merely a marketing programme, it should be perceived as a company-wide programme affecting all points of customer contact in the total customer experience. E-CRM provides electronic or Web intermediation for the customer experience, but responsibility for the quality of the experience at the contact point remains with the appropriate entity. Therefore all customer-facing departments should be brought in from the very beginning of the project in order to get their view, experience and commitment to the success of the e-CRM project. Without their commitment, an e-CRM programme will either become an isolated programme with limited value for customers or it will fail. The earlier all customer-facing departments are involved, the higher the chance of a successful company-wide programme; beyond that, their contribution to the project will be to provide content, features and integration with their back-end systems. Of course, IT should also be involved from the outset to make sure that the IT infrastructure and the choices of application software and services support the e-CRM model.

Project organisation and decision making

Already at the planning stage and before implementation, a number of functions should be represented in the project and form a team around the project leader. The same person, depending on the enterprise and its organisational format, could represent one or more functions. The nature and size of the project will influence how large the project team should be and the percentage of the time spent on it by members.

Here we would like to point out that the *sponsors* (high-level company management), although not part of the project team, have the role of monitoring the project and keeping it on track by representing the higher-order goals and by funding it.

Below are the functions that we suggest should be represented on the team:

- *E-CRM project leader*: to drive and manage the overall e-CRM project, including project planning and control, budgeting, resource planning, co-ordination and decision making, all typical tasks of a project manager. After-wards, when e-CRM is running, this person could take on responsibility for the total customer experience by monitoring the contribution of customer-facing entities to e-CRM, by publishing measurements and results of customer activity on the Web, online product sales and online customer surveys.
- *Programme management representatives for each department involved*: to represent the department's specific needs in the

project; to represent and to drive the project's needs in their department; to negotiate internal service-level agreements. Members would come from departments such as marketing, sales centres, service and support centres and all departments in direct contact with customers. Members would also come from *regional and country departments* to represent country- and customer-specific needs such as localisation and legislation and to represent the project in their country.

- *Resale channels*: these should be invited to participate and agree on the services they will provide to end-users in the context of the total customer experience.
- *IT, Web and network project management*: to represent IT infrastructure capabilities; to evaluate feasibility and costs; to contribute to vendor software evaluation; to design, implement and support specific solutions required by the project.
- *Content management and competition research*: while content should be provided by each of the customer-facing entities, co-ordination of the process and commissioning of new content should be managed at the project level. This requires the organisation to stay up to date on what is going on in electronic media, learning what the competition does on the Internet in order to keep abreast and provide the content and services that customers expect.
- *Legal*: last but not least, there is a need to check if the e-CRM concept and operating practices meet the legal requirements of data protection and customer privacy and to prepare and maintain the privacy policy and privacy statement.

A cross-section of *customers* from key target groups, while not members of the project team, should be invited to participate in the evaluation of the concept and in testing the implementation. Their feedback is essential to the successful outcome of the project. Similarly, *super-users* of e-CRM from customer-facing departments should be invited to contribute their experience during the test phase.

Every project that cuts across organisational lines must apply a transparent decision-making process in order to function. The decision-making process will certainly be influenced by the culture of the enterprise, but the role of project leader will be key in preparing the decisions that must be reached by consensus, making day-to-day decisions for the team and escalating difficult cases to the sponsors. Often the sponsors will form a *steering committee* that has the final decision-making power on major decisions for the project.

Prepare project performance measures

E-CRM is about people and technology serving customers to build relationships with them and to earn their loyalty. If we are looking for measures that are aligned with the role and purpose of e-CRM, we should be thinking of measuring how well the project implementation serves the customers: how satisfied they are with the service, what their preferences are in terms of traditional versus electronic media, how the new services are affecting their productivity and their quality of life, what features and content they prefer, what changes they would like to see.

Those who are responsible for web features, for the private area or for outbound e-mail newsletters should ask customers about their experience with the service they receive and learn how to improve it. Collecting customer feedback, either through customer satisfaction surveys or through online interviews, should be part of daily life. One of the measures could well be the number of solicited comments received per month, another could be the trend in customer satisfaction. These are measures that encourage e-marketing people to keep in touch with real customers. However, they are not short-term measures: customer satisfaction measures tend to evolve relatively slowly over months and years, therefore it would be unrealistic and unfair to set aggressive measures with regard to improved customer satisfaction in the first six months after introducing the first phase of e-CRM services. A one- to two-year period seems to be more realistic.

Web activity measures, such as the number of hits on a specific page of your web site, tell you just that – they don't say anything about whether customers found what they were looking for. The trend in number of hits may be construed as an indicator of customer interest in the content of the page, up or down, but in the end it cannot be easily converted into economic gain or loss; activity measures are like advertising measures in this respect.

On the other hand, if the number of incoming product support calls into your call centre drops by 20 per cent three months after introducing the self-help feature and by another 30 per cent six months thereafter, this is a clear result and tells you two facts: (a) customers accept and are using the self-help feature; and (b) your call centre workload is coming down and with it its related costs.

Process measures that assess the efficiency of e-marketing campaigns can also be envisaged when the e-CRM implementation is running, for example 'send e-mail to targets – clickthrough rate – purchase rate'.

It therefore makes sense to plan for measures of economic return based on the impact that the e-CRM implementation will have on the productivity of the organisation. But again, expectations must be set within a realistic time frame.

IT infrastructure performance measures should be agreed with the IT department or IT services supplier: site availability or up-time, system response measures ('response to customer in less than x seconds'), data integrity, security, back-up, service response time and so on. The e-CRM infrastructure should always be available.

Plan the investment

Measures of return on investment, like those discussed above, will of course have a direct impact on the investment plan. If at the planning stage the web self-help feature can be shown to reduce costs or improve the productivity of the call centre within the first year, the initial funding for the self-help project should not be too difficult to obtain. If it can be shown that e-mail marketing brings down the cost per mail shot and increases the productivity of direct response selling, compared to traditional direct mail, it should not be that difficult to get funding approved for an e-mail solution.

Each feature could be separately justified, but it is important not to engage in piecemeal funding of separate e-CRM islands, because you will not have the critical mass to invest in the customer information database and in the information management processes that support the e-CRM environment. Plan the entire e-CRM environment, including the supporting infrastructure, and introduce it step by step. Do not only consider the features that bring the most value to the enterprise, but also those that bring the most value to customers: consistent experience with superior customer service leads to customer loyalty measured in repeat, profitable business. E-CRM is not about short-term economic gain, but about long-term customer relationships and profitable growth.

Concept and design
Define the target customers

To maintain the entire e-CRM project in focus you need to concentrate on defined customers. You may choose to start with your most valued customers as a customer segment, but of course you could select other customer segments based on your business situation. It is clearly important to involve all customer-facing departments in the definition of the targeted segments. Without knowing whom you will serve you will not be able to develop the right personalisation features.

Evaluate the customer experience at all the critical points of contact

Investigate all the different ways in which customers get in touch with your enterprise during the buying process. For each of these points of contact, see if they can be served through electronic services on the Web or via e-mail. This is a base for examining possible interactive features: what do your customers need most from your company? What information, what service, what else? This does not mean that you would replace all human contacts by the Web. It means, for example, that in addition to a phone-in service, you could offer self-help on the Web.

Don't force customers to switch to Web-based services if they prefer contacting the call centre. Give them the opportunity to try Web services through some incentive and let them decide. They will move if they experience quality, convenience and speed.

Know your competition and learn from your customers

It is always wise to keep an eye on the competition and see what they offer or advertise in terms of customer services on the Web. It is not too difficult to observe what they do in the public domain. However, as soon as your competition offers access to a private, personalised web site, you lose visibility and the only way to find out what the site offers is to ask a customer who uses it.

Do not try to replicate what the competition does. By the time you get there they will be ahead of you again. Try to give something better from the beginning. Prepare a detailed list of what you will offer to your customers, including a personalised web site, multi-channel communication, e-mail marketing services or even personalised call centre contacts with Web collaboration if appropriate. Take your service list to the target group and let the customers tell you what they like and don't like and what their preferences and priorities are. Find out what your customers value the most from your competitors' services and from your offer and what they miss or would like to see. The chance is high that you will come back with a huge list of features, services and benefits that you could in theory offer to your customers. The challenge is to prioritise them, which is not an easy task.

Our proposal is to rank the services according to four prioritisation criteria: (a) benefits to your customer; (b) value to your company; (c) short-term implementation feasibility; and (d) alignment with the vision. The best-scoring services in the rank-ordered list could be included in the implementation plan.

This is much easier to say than to do it, but when did a me-too strategy benefit customers? Why should your customers stay with you if they can get something better from the competition? Or why should your competitors' customers defect?

Draft your privacy policy

By writing down a privacy policy at the planning stage you will, at the same time, have a good tool to determine early enough the features you will be able to implement, as well as those you cannot or do not want to implement. There may be a feature that ranks really high in terms of benefits both to you and to your customers, but that cannot be implemented in some countries due to customer privacy regulations. If you had caught this fact after implementation you would have wasted time and resources and missed a chance to change the concept early enough so that it fits the regulations.

Describe your overall concept

This is the time to tie everything together and document the overall concept. This is a major task because you must describe all the features, processes and benefits that you will offer your customers in the first and following releases of the e-CRM environment. What kind of personalisation will you offer? On what profile data will you base your services? What will the integration with your back-end systems look like? Here you describe all the elements of your registration, profiling, service and personalisation processes and systems and prepare a set of pictures or diagrams that illustrate how customers will experience your e-CRM environment.

Check again with your customers

Explain to your customers how you incorporated their feedback in the design and what you plan to implement when. From your customers' perspective, your e-CRM concept must be easy to understand and bring clear benefits. If you find it difficult to communicate, you may have to revisit the design. For example, if the user interface is too difficult to explain, does it mean it will be too difficult to use?

Don't be afraid of getting destructive comments from your customers at this stage – it will only help you improve your concept and focus your resources on the right implementation. Some customers will not be willing to spend that much time with you going over your plan and concept, but some will. Some are genuinely pleased to be involved in such a task. They can express what is important to them, and if they see that their inputs are taken into consideration and they are influencing the design, there is a higher chance that they will become early users of the planned e-CRM services. Involving customers appropriately in the development phase is a win–win situation.

Set realistic plans and expectations

As you need to foresee a phased implementation of the e-CRM project, it is now time to plan the overall project: timetables, milestones, budget, resources, tests and releases by phase. The danger you could run into at this time is to over-promise in terms of expected results and return on investment. The project sponsors tend to forget the niceties of the customer service features, but remember very well deadlines and ROI figures. Don't plan for a step-like improvement in customer usage or in productivity gains. It takes time for customers to learn about the new services and to make use of them regularly.

A successful e-CRM project will extensively communicate to customers the progress and the milestones achieved in order to prepare them for the upcoming services and invite them to register and use these. If you plan and execute your e-CRM project well, customer satisfaction will increase, productivity will improve and costs in specific areas will go down – just don't set expectations too high for the first year.

Define content processes and responsibilities

When you have drawn a picture of the customer experience with your e-CRM environment, you can take that picture and identify all the individual features and content items visible to your customers. For all of these features and content items you now design what should happen in the background to make the features work and deliver the content.

As we said earlier, content management is pivotal to a successful outcome. Processes must be defined and content responsibilities assigned: what content goes where; how often the content will change; what events trigger content updates; who provides what content items; how you approve and decide what content goes where; who checks for outdated content on the Web and removes it; how you administer the private area content; if you offer multilingual content, who co-ordinates the different language correspondents and content providers. This is not unlike an editorial task and will require oversight throughout the life of the e-CRM implementation.

Define feature processes and responsibilities

After evaluating and selecting the right solutions and tools to build your e-CRM environment, you need to assign responsibilities for every feature offered to customers. Define who is responsible for which feature: for design integration with back-end systems; for interoperability among applications and solutions. You also need to agree on an escalation process when a feature does not perform in production. In summary, for every feature there is someone responsible to make it happen. This is especially important when you are planning and designing an e-CRM concept that involves people from different departments – it reaffirms organisational commitment to the project.

Check with legal (again)

Are all the aspects of your e-CRM implementation meeting the legal restrictions and regulations that apply in the countries you intend to serve? Are you allowed to store customer data in a database? Are you allowed to transfer customer data cross the Atlantic into a common customer database? Are you allowed to analyse customer data? Do you know which features or services the customer must explicitly approve? These are just a few of the items to check, as well as the final privacy policy statement and disclaimers.

Build and test

Build mock-ups and test them with customers

You have completed the design phase: the features, application interfaces, batch and online processes are designed. At this stage, it would be wise to build screen mock-ups of the customer user interfaces, as customers will experience them after release. Check them out with customers now and see if any changes are necessary. It is much more efficient to introduce changes before building the applications than later, after the first development and implementation. Also let customers check the navigation to see if it is intuitive and easy to handle.

Build the system

As we do not focus on the IT aspects of e-CRM in this book, we will not drill into the IT project implementation steps that will bring the e-CRM services online. The build (or buy and customise) phase will cover all aspects: application(s), network, infrastructure and integration. With your IT department you will be closely monitoring developments in this phase to make sure that what is under construction and is later delivered meets the design objectives. It is common practice to run a fully functional internal test (also called an alpha test) and make corrections where necessary before releasing the first implementation for external testing by selected customers (the beta test).

Security is not an option

All sensitive data (both customer data and enterprise data) must be protected and secured. There can be no compromise on this. Verify that this is the case for the first release.

Educate your people and manage the change

This aspect of the build phase is often misunderstood and neglected. Plenty of training should and often is given at the system level: how to use the new 'machine', how to feed it with content, how to manage the process interfaces between front end and back end, how to extract reports etc., all the aspects of how to operate the system once it is up and running.

However, what is needed, in addition to system level training, is education on the impact that the new e-CRM environment will have on the quality of customer relationships through better services and higher productivity. Depending on the specific situation and experience of your enterprise, the new e-CRM environment may require additional education in customer orientation for the people involved. It may require refocusing of the different customer-facing departments on customers without abandoning their productivity measures. It may require modifying or eliminating existing processes and practices to leverage the functionality offered by the new e-CRM environment. It may require reorganising or merging certain functions. It may require changing individual and organisational performance measures. It *will* require propagating the early vision of the project to motivate and mobilise employees.

This is because you are introducing change and will need to manage change. On page 44 we used the analogy of an iceberg to illustrate the hidden aspects of change. Deepest down below the surface is the behaviour aspect. Behaviour doesn't change without changes in values and measures. A new vision transmits new values and new measures redirect behaviour.

An enterprise that is very much product oriented has difficulty focusing on customers because its values and measures of performance are essentially product and productivity. An enterprise that is customer oriented still worries about products and productivity, but remains focused on customers because its value and measures are customer service, customer satisfaction and quality of service. E-CRM is about enhancing the quality of the total customer experience with your enterprise – it is up to you to determine what changes it will bring and how to manage those changes.

Run the beta test

Has your system passed the alpha test? Now let a selected group of customers test it in what is called the beta test. Let them 'test drive' your implementation: is it really easy to use? Do all the features deliver what you and your customers expected? Is the performance acceptable? Do the customers understand the user interface, wording and content? Is the navigation intuitive and easy to follow? Very often companies let their customers test only parts or specific features of a new design. A real beta test should cover all aspects of the system: all features and processes have to pass the test, including front-end to back-end integration.

Single features should be tested ('if you click here, then that screen should appear'), but the more important tests concern multi-step tasks defined by customers, such as 'I need specific product information', 'I want to place a service request', 'I want to subscribe to the newsletter', 'I want to unsubscribe from the newsletter', 'I want to change my personal profile data'. But there are also more complex tasks that should be tested by customers in a beta-test environment. For example: send them your first newsletter and ask them to follow an embedded link. Let them order an item, check the order status, subscribe for e-mail notification and receive an e-mail once the order status changes.

In all these cases the customers describe their experiences and you collect their inputs. The idea behind these examples is to not test isolated features but to test processes and scenarios, as they are likely to happen once the services are online. You could also ask customers to evaluate your planned communication messages about the new services and see if you establish the correct expectations.

If during the tests the customers navigated differently to the way you expected, don't try to show them how they could do it better. You might have a chance of convincing your beta-test customers, but you will not have a chance to convince all the other visitors coming to your web site in the future. The better way is to discover what needs to be changed (and hopefully improved) in the navigation or wording so that the tasks will be easier to perform.

When customers are willing to set aside time to beta test your environment, you have responsibility to set the right expectations: explain what the test is for, in what phase of the development of the e-CRM environment you are and how you will deal with their feedback. Customers should not get the impression that you are ready to make all the changes they propose. Because of project timetables or technical constraints you may be able to deal with only some of the proposed changes in the first release of the e-CRM environment. Nevertheless, they should learn about the changes that were introduced as a consequence of their feedback – they will appreciate this.

Test performance and go live

Performance is a key success factor of any Internet service. Before you release your e-CRM services, the web site and all the features should be tested under full load to see how the system performs when a maximum number of users visit the site and use its features. When you later announce the new services to a large number of customers, the chance is high that your site will experience peak load conditions at some time as your customers (and most certainly your competitors) check out what you announced. It would leave a very bad first impression if your e-CRM environment slowed down to a crawl or crashed under the load.

The next step is to get sign-off from every member of the project team responsible for major parts of the e-CRM environment and from the sponsors or decision makers – whatever your signoff strategy. It is finally time to bring the system live and to invite your customers to experience it.

Promote your new services

Now that you have system performance and a (hopefully) bug-free environment, how will customers learn about the great features you are offering? How will you invite them to try the new services? You need to promote the new services. The approach is pretty much like running a new product campaign, where the target groups are those that were previously defined for the e-CRM project. Customer communications are an integral part of the plan and you want to communicate the features and their benefits to your customers.

If you already have a web site, you can announce your new services there. However, you can use any appropriate communication channel, depending on the size of the target audience, from targeted e-mail messages to press releases.

You can also associate with your communication plan those business partners that co-operated with you in the e-CRM strategy, perhaps by placing articles in their newsletters or magazines.

If your first target is the high-value customer segment, personalised letters offering the new services will make a great impression, particularly if you combine them with pre-registration as we discussed on page 65. It would be even better if top management signed the invitation letter, stressing how important it is for the enterprise to serve customers better.

Customers who participated in surveys and tests will greatly appreciate a letter saying 'Thank you and here it is'.

Customer service phase

Measure and improve

Run the measurement tools to track what your customers do in your web site, what content they are looking for, what search criteria they enter. Track how often they read your e-mail, how often they click on embedded links, how often they use the self-service features and so on. In addition, survey your customers to learn how they rank your services compared to your competition and how satisfied they are with what you offer. Learn how they value specific services, if you are deficient in certain areas or even if you are over-supplied in others. Use the feedback to improve your services.

Everybody gets customer feedback

All departments and functions that contribute content, online services or support to the e-CRM solution should get customer feedback on how they are doing, what is working well and what is not and what needs improvement. For example, the content providers should get feedback on whether their content has been found and accessed. If content providers learn that their documents are not accessed (read), this could mean that their content is not interesting enough to attract visitors or that it is hard for visitors to find it. In either case, some improvements should be introduced, for example provide more interesting content; or improve the search algorithm/key words or the user interface/links that lead to the content.

Continuously improve

You may use regular interviews or structured questionnaires to find out if you meet customer expectations and determine how you can improve. An e-CRM solution is not a static operating environment that is defined once in the design and build phase and doesn't change thereafter. The objective after going online is always to try to improve and serve customers better. The competitive environment of the Web doesn't leave you any other choice.

Once online there are two areas to focus on:

- the current services with the current features and content. The challenge here is to continuously improve the existing features and the content so that the e-CRM environment continues to satisfy customers.
- New areas of customer service not yet provided to customers: this is especially important to stay ahead of competition and to attract new customers over the years.

Keep management informed

Don't expect your board of directors to log in regularly to explore your e-CRM environment and praise the great and wonderful things going on there. Keep them appraised, if they are the sponsors, of the progress you make in order to maintain their commitment and the funding needed for the next steps you are planning. Bring them survey results, customer testimonials and anecdotes, give them guided tours. Demonstrate how the site protects customer data privacy and show how e-CRM helps increase productivity and other ROI measures. By enlisting the support of other departments involved in the project.

Finally convince them that e-CRM goes beyond short-term gains and that, when properly deployed, it can help sustain profitable customer relationships, with corresponding benefits for the customers and for the enterprise, over the long term.

Key message

You now have a framework and an action plan for bringing e-CRM successfully into your enterprise. You can see both the benefits and the challenges – but the benefits captured by the vision can be far superior to the challenges posed by the implementation. It is now your decision: it's up to you.

Creating more customer value

CHAPTER 9

Overview

In this final chapter we present some counterintuitive ideas:

- How to create more customer value by handing power back to your customers.
- Sponsored online communities as a business model for gaining customer knowledge and earning customer trust.

From four Ps to four Cs

Most marketers in the past grew accustomed to the four Ps of marketing: product, price, place (or distribution) and promotion. These were comfortable and easy to remember, they were like the four points on a compass and gave direction to the strategic as well as the tactical activities of marketing in an enterprise. However, the digital economy has shifted the focus of businesses on to the customer and is calling attention to other reference points.

In *The Essentials of e-Business Leadership*, Keyur Patel and Mary Pat McCarthy refer to six aspects of the business-wide, digital transformation of the enterprise as it focuses on customers: culture, collaboration, community, cost, content and commerce. Similarly, from the marketing perspective, the digital economy is causing an almost symmetrical transformation of the 4 Ps of traditional marketing into the 4 Cs of e-marketing: customer, content, commerce and community.

As the Web increasingly becomes the marketing platform of choice for many enterprises, those more likely to benefit from the available technologies and leverage their presence on the Web to their advantage are the ones that are truly customer focused and that continuously add value to their relationship with the customers. Consequently, more customer value will need to be created along the customer intimacy dimension or value discipline as competing enterprises close the gap on operational excellence and on product/service leadership.

The most obvious strategy, in terms of creating more value along the intimacy dimension, is to integrate all of the functions of the enterprise around the customer, so that customer focus is not only understood but practised with passion by all the customer-facing activities of the enterprise (front office) and supported by all the back-office functions. This is largely what we have covered in this book when discussing the total customer experience and showing how content personalisation, through the private area of the web site and coupled to back-end integration, can provide unmatched service to customers.

While not trivial in terms of implementation challenges, this strategy is plausible and intuitively acceptable because it leaves the initiative in the hands of the enterprise. The mechanisms put in place are there to respond to customer needs, but marketing is still doing its job of crafting and communicating value propositions, making offers to customers, closing business and soliciting customer feedback to improve the enterprise's value added.

A less intuitive strategy is to give more power back to the customers. Not that customers have been standing back on this issue: they have progressively taken more power in their hands as the Web has effectively levelled the playing field between buyers and sellers by making available, at practically no cost, the information that buyers need to make informed decisions. This is happening in the e-commerce world both in business to consumer, through electronic group buying where communities of individuals combine their purchasing power to drive down prices, and in business to business, where e-commerce exchanges allow buyers, for a fee, to get the lowest possible prices through competitive bidding among suppliers, typically in the context of low-complexity products. In industries where suppliers are fragmented, competing enterprises are forming buyers' communities or trading consortia to gain the benefits of their pooled purchasing power. This power shift is caused by the formation of online communities of individuals or of enterprises that share a common interest and together can achieve an economic benefit.

Online communities

Online communities are not new. They started as conversation and conferencing environments for thinkers in all walks of life, exclusively for intellectual and creative purposes. The best known probably is The Well (www.well.com), which traces its origins back to 1985. Some communities took on a commercial orientation and evolved to focused, specialised e-marketplaces such as www.sciquest.com in the scientific sector, or gave way to commercial 'megamalls' hosted by online service providers with thousands of stores and millions of products, such as www.wholesalehub.com.

Communities on the Web have come about because most people want to learn, be accepted and taken seriously. The word gets out that there is a specific site where a certain discussion goes on, where personal or business contacts can be made – visitors are attracted and may wind up joining the action and eventually become members of the community.

Online communities generate new information because they revolve around a particular interest, hobby or professional task. As members share information and create knowledge by interacting with one another, they also add content to the community site. In so doing they attract other visitors, build traffic and more knowledge, and the communities become 'deep wells of knowledge'.

Communities also generate their own loyalty because members develop the habit of returning to the site over and over again and develop a sense of ownership, particularly if they are actively involved in discussions or in sharing information.

Communities can also help develop the business of enterprises and merchants present on sites that have a commercial orientation. Once members become used to the site they become comfortable with making purchases there rather than venturing into unknown territory. They develop trust, which leads to more business.

If we look at these developments from the relationship marketing viewpoint, we can say that there are two trends. On one hand, businesses seek to utilise online interactive services to establish deeper and broader relationships with their customers and to increase understanding of their needs. On the other, consumers seek to satisfy their basic social need for communication and information in a more convenient manner through the Web, not limited by the constraints of 'same time, same geography'.

The convergence of these two trends creates an opportunity for enterprises to sponsor focused 'customer communities' where they and their business partners can expand their online relationships as well as their business with customers. Sponsored online communities can feature specialised e-marketplaces and syndicated services such as news feeds, special event productions, editorial features, features such as 'how to' articles, chat rooms, marketing promotions, affiliate merchant offers and the like.

Sponsored online communities

Sponsored online communities are the expression of an e-marketing strategy where power is effectively handed back to customers. Community sites are not corporate sites. They can reflect the corporate image of the sponsoring brand through the look and feel of the web site design and they may well have a commercial orientation, but they are built around the common needs and interests of their members. The enterprises that sponsor online communities have a more subtle and unassertive presence and seek to understand and satisfy the interests of customers rather than pushing product-specific content, as they typically do in their corporate web sites.

Sponsored online communities thrive best when sponsoring enterprises relinquish some control to their customers in order to receive candid and constructive criticism. This may seem counterintuitive, particularly to those who think that marketing's job is to broadcast good news and filter out bad news, much less to let candid criticism openly appear in chat rooms or bulletin boards. That is mass-marketing thinking, but in relationship marketing every criticism is an opportunity to serve the customer better.

Acknowledging criticism and resolving issues raised by customers can have a more positive effect on brand awareness and customer loyalty than incentive-based schemes. There is gold in every criticism or complaint – that is how enterprises can learn quickly ways to improve their offer and their customer service compared to competition and they can foster customer loyalty to their brand.

Customers would rather exchange information with one another and gain knowledge by interacting in a friendly community environment than search for information in a corporate site, where they would be given a corporate sales pitch that they would not find credible in any case. In a sponsored online community model, the sponsoring enterprise would, of course, also gain knowledge about product usage, product competitiveness, quality of service and the like, but it would do so unobtrusively by monitoring bulletin boards as well as by moderating chat rooms.

From the perspective of this model, the main criteria for a successful sponsored community are: distinctive focus or field of interest, appreciation and encouragement of content generated by community members, capacity to integrate and communicate relevant content, professionally managed event production and moderated discussion environment, commercial orientation, commercial partnerships with complementary vendors on the site and, of course, promotion of the community site.

In a community web site the primary measure of success is its 'stickiness', that is, the amount of time that individual community members spend on the site in community events, chat rooms etc., rather than the number of clicks, individual visits or other web traffic and advertising measures. Community members will regularly log in and stay online if they find content and programming on the site that is interesting, useful and stimulating and offers that are appealing. For this to happen, the community sponsor or builder should target a specific yet sufficiently large market segment where customers and prospects, existing or prospective community members, have strong common interests and a personal or even emotional identification with their field of interest. The community should benefit from a network of relevant content providers and from professional communication and programming skills, and should have access to a network of complementary business partners and merchants and to a reliable e-CRM and e-commerce infrastructure.

The expected benefits for the sponsoring enterprise are: increased brand awareness, an online community-based marketing opportunity, the on-going acquisition of customer feedback, reduced new customer acquisition costs and increased customer loyalty. Community members would benefit from a welcoming and friendly environment, valuable information by field of interest, a variety of interactive programming and dialogue with other community members. Partners and advertisers would find a community of engaged viewers, a targetable audience, a critical mass of traffic, variety in programming and an effective branding venue.

From the financial viewpoint, a sponsored online community represents an interesting marketing initiative because it could become entirely self-funding after the initial investment by the sponsor. The income generated through commissions on e-commerce transactions and, to a lesser extent, through advertising fees from business partners and affiliated merchants could cover the operating expenses (promotion of the site, content development, programming, management and maintenance) and even return the original investment if the site can attract over time a large enough and growing community of members. Different business model scenarios reflecting different assumptions and experiences can be built to predict the occurrence of a break-even point, but of course the sponsor would have to assume the risk that scenario predictions and actual performance can be widely different.

The sponsored online community model may not be the last model in the ever-changing kaleidoscope of the e-economy, but it challenges some of the best entrenched paradigms. By handing power back to customers, enterprises gain the underlying knowledge accumulated in the deep wells of the community – knowledge that can be turned into competitive advantage. But, more importantly, they gain the trust of members and trust is the common currency of business.

The world is changing – change means opportunity

Just as in the past all major technical innovations in communications – printed media, telephone, radio and television – have changed people's way of acquiring information, communicating with one another, working and doing business at a distance, so the Internet has changed and will continue to change the way people acquire information, communicate, work and do business across the boundaries of 'same space, same time'. In the past, communications innovations provided better conduits or pipelines for linking people in different physical locations, but the Internet has moved its value beyond that of a communications pipeline – it has become a destination.

More of our personal and work time will be spent in the virtual space represented by the Web. Without philosophising or romanticising about cyberspace, a science-fiction term from the 1980s, the reality is that there is no way back, there is only a way forward. Across industries many enterprises have seen the vast stores of wealth that represent global consumer communities in cyberspace and gone after them in 'gold rush' style, armed with the picks and shovels of the new technologies. And many learned the hard lesson that the technologies by themselves or a '.com' after their name are not a guarantee of success.

Customer focus, understanding of customers' needs and lifestyles, respect of customers' privacy and a desire to satisfy individual customer preferences are what make the difference between lasting business success and irrelevance and eventual failure on the Internet.

In this book we wanted to bring you some principles and methods for how an enterprise can benefit from recent web technologies and developments. We did not intend to project future possibilities or describe sophisticated new technologies and trends. Instead, we looked at customer needs and how existing technologies, together with front-office and back-end strategies, can help you satisfy those needs – today, profitably and reliably. Our goal was to encourage you to combine the strength of your existing customer knowledge with the power and flexibility offered by the new electronic media and to help you see how to build a customer-oriented, enterprise-wide e-CRM environment, an environment where change is irreversible, but where the opportunity to combine web technologies with customer focus to build lasting profitable businesses is clearly there. We hope that we have achieved that goal.

BIBLIOGRAPHY

Allen, Cliff, Kania, Deborah and Yaeckel, Beth (1998) *Guide to One-to-One Web Marketing*, John Wiley & Sons.

Amor, Daniel (2000) *The E-business (R)evolution, Living and Working in an Interconnected World*, Prentice-Hall.

Godin, Seth (1999) *Permission Marketing*, Simon & Schuster.

Gulati, Ranjay and Govino, Jason (2000) 'Get the right mix of bricks and clicks', *Harvard Business Review*, May–Jun.

Hagel, John, III and Armstrong, Arthur G. (1997) *net.gain*, Harvard Business School Press.

Janal, Daniel S. (2000) *Dan Janal's Guide to Marketing on the Internet*, John Wiley & Sons.

Kinnard, Shannon (1999) *Marketing with E-Mail*, Maximum Press.

McKenna, Regis (1991) *Relationship Marketing*, Addison-Wesley.

Patel, Keyur and McCarthy, Mary Pat (2000) *Digital Transformation: the Essentials of e-Business Leadership*, McGraw-Hill.

Peppers, Don and Rogers, Martha (1997) *Enterprise One to One*, Doubleday.

Peppers, Don and Rogers, Martha (1999) *The One-to-One Fieldbook*, Doubleday.

Reichheld, Frederick F. (1996) *The Loyalty Effect*, Harvard Business School Press.

Reichheld, Frederick (1996a) 'Learning from customer defections', *Harvard Business Review*, Mar.–Apr.

Schwartz, Evan (1997) *Webonomics*, Broadway Books.

Seybold, Patricia B. (1998) *Customers.com*, Times Business.

Sterne, Jim and Priore, Anthony (2000) *Email Marketing*, John Wiley & Sons.

Treacy, Michael and Wiersema, Frederick D. (1997) *The Discipline of Market Leaders: Choose Your Customers, Narrow Your Focus, Dominate Your Market*, Addison-Wesley.

Vavra, Terry G. (1995) *Aftermarketing*, Irwin.

Ward, Scott, Light, Larry and Goldstine, Jonathan (1999) 'Brands for high-tech managers', *Harvard Business Review*, Jul.–Aug.